imagism

A CHAPTER FOR THE
HISTORY OF MODERN POETRY

imagism

A CHAPTER FOR THE HISTORY OF MODERN POETRY

By STANLEY K. Coffman, JR.

OCTAGON BOOKS

A DIVISION OF FARRAR, STRAUS AND GIROUX

New York   1977

Copyright 1951 by the University of Oklahoma Press

Reprinted 1972
by special arrangement with the University of Oklahoma Press
Second Octagon printing 1977

OCTAGON BOOKS
A DIVISION OF FARRAR, STRAUS & GIROUX, INC.
19 Union Square West
New York, N.Y. 10003

Library of Congress Cataloging in Publication Data

Coffman, Stanley K
    Imagism; a chapter for the history of modern poetry.

    Reprint of the 1st ed.
    Includes bibliographical references.
    1. Imagist poetry—History and criticism. 2. American poetry
    —20th century—History and criticism. 3. English poetry—
    20th century—History and criticism. I. Title.
PS310.15C6   1972   821'.9'1209   72-4262
ISBN 0-374-91793-0

Manufactured by Braun-Brumfield, Inc.
Ann Arbor, Michigan
Printed in the United States of America

To my mother and father

Acknowledgments

A MONG the most important of my source materials were
several collections of letters (most of them as yet
unpublished) written by the Imagist poets during
the period with which this book deals. I am especially grateful to the following for permission to quote
passages from their correspondence: Mrs. Hilda Aldington,
the executors of Miss Amy Lowell's estate, Dr. William
Carlos Williams, Richard Aldington, and D. D. Paige for
Ezra Pound. Before his death, John Gould Fletcher not
only gave his approval to quotations I wished to use but
contributed information which helped fill out the picture
presented here. Since these materials were not available in
published form, I have not given any documentation for
them except where it was necessary to identify the writer
of a letter.

I should also like to thank those now responsible for
these collections, which are invaluable to any study of contemporary American poetry: Charles Abbott, curator, and
Miss Janet Brown of the Lockwood Memorial Library,
University of Buffalo (mainly for the letters from Pound
and from Mrs. Aldington to Dr. Williams); Charles Jack-
son, curator of the Houghton Library, Harvard Univer-

sity (for letters from the Imagists and others to Miss Amy Lowell); Mrs. Judith Bond, curator of the Harriet Monroe Collection, University of Chicago (for letters from the Imagists and others to, Miss Harriet Monroe). To Miss Eugenia Patterson of the New York Public Library I owe a special debt for her gracious assistance in making available to me extensive collections of "little magazines" in that library.

I am grateful to the following publishers for kindly allowing me to use the materials noted: The Macmillan Company for permission to quote from "To a Snail" by Marianne Moore *(Selected Poems,* copyright 1935 by Marianne Moore) and from "The Magi" by William Butler Yeats *(Responsibilities,* copyright 1916); Houghton Mifflin Company for quotations from *Some Imagist Poets,* 1915, 1916, and from Amy Lowell's *Men, Women, and Ghosts* (copyright 1916 by Amy Lowell); Harcourt Brace and Company for the lines from "Preludes," by T. S. Eliot *(Collected Poems,* copyright 1936) and from T. E. Hulme's *Speculations* (copyright 1924); New Directions for Dr. Williams' "Between Walls" *(Selected Poems,* copyright 1949 by William Carlos Williams) and for Ezra Pound's "In a Station of the Metro," "Phanopoeia," and "Heather" *(Personae,* copyright 1926 by Ezra Pound); Harcourt, Brace and Company for passages from *The Letters of Ezra Pound 1907–1941;* Rinehart and Company, Inc., for the passage from John Gould Fletcher's *Selected Poems* (copyright 1938 by John Gould Fletcher); Liveright Publishing Corporation for "Oread" from the *Collected Poems of H. D.* (copyright 1925 by Boni and Liveright, Inc.); Faber and Faber, Ltd., for passages from Michael Roberts' *T. E. Hulme* (copyright 1938).

ACKNOWLEDGEMENTS

Grateful acknowledgment is due the following for permission to quote from prose works on which they hold the copyright: Constable and Co. Ltd.; Crown Publishers; Eyre and Spottiswoode; Faber and Faber, Ltd.; Farrar and Rinehart; Harcourt, Brace and Company; Houghton Mifflin Company; Liveright Publishing Corporation; The Macmillan Company; Methuen and Co., Ltd.; G. P. Putnam's Sons; The Viking Press.

Finally, I want to express my sincere gratitude to Frederick J. Hoffman who patiently and carefully guided me in the early stages of my work; to Victor A. Elconin, who read the final drafts and made suggestions for improvement—all of which were incorporated; and to my wife, whose unfailing interest in the book was a source of en couragement which can only too inadequately be expressed here. None of them is responsible for whatever shortcomings it may be found to have; these are mine.

STANLEY K. COFFMAN, JR.

Norman, Oklahoma
January 10, 1951

Contents

imagism

A CHAPTER FOR THE
HISTORY OF MODERN POETRY

The Imagist Movement, 1912-14

I MAGISM refers to the theory and practice of a group of
poets who, between 1912 and 1917, joined in reaction
against the careless technique and extra-poetic values
of much nineteenth-century verse. Through their anthologies and manifestoes the Imagists gained an appearance
of unity convincing enough to establish them as a "school."
The appearance, however, is misleading, and Imagism is
not easy to define. It is possible to suggest certain characteristics of rhythm and style that occur regularly in Imagist
poems, but practice varied so greatly among the contributors
to the anthologies that it is necessary to describe a given
poem not as "Imagist," but as Imagist "in the manner of"
a particular poet. And the statements of principle published
in the manifestoes were general enough that they are of little
use in providing a definition of exactly what distinguishes
an Imagist poem from any other.

At the same time, there is a sense in which Imagism may
be defined satisfactorily and inclusively, for it was not just
a matter of technique. It was also an attitude toward the
nature and function of poetry, an attitude whose significance
extends beyond its use in explaining the formal qualities
of a special kind of verse. What held these poets together

was less a way of writing than a feeling, seldom clearly articulated, about what poetry should be and do in our culture. Their "school" expressed a climate of opinion, something that was "in the air," and it is this, primarily, which makes definition possible. Defined in these terms—that is, in its historical context—Imagism has its fullest meaning; it was the first attempt by contemporary poets to formulate a change of direction that would mark them as contemporary, and an understanding of Imagism is important for explaining, in part, the direction taken by poetry since 1912.

It began as a publicity stunt which circumstances soon proved to have a value beyond its immediate purpose. In the spring of 1912, Ezra Pound was working with the first of an impressive series of "discoveries" among unpublished or unrecognized writers—Hilda Doolittle and Richard Aldington—and one day, after studying some of their poems, he announced to them, significantly and with evident approval, that they were *Imagistes*.[1] What the word meant to him at this time would be difficult to say, and he seemed in no hurry to extend its circulation, though it appeared again a few months later in a letter to Harriet Monroe, now descriptive of one of his own poems—"an over-elaborate post-Browning 'Imagiste' affair."[2] Not until October and the publication of his *Ripostes* were *Les Imagistes* presented to the public, and then quite casually: *Ripostes* included "The Complete Poetical Works of T. E. Hulme" (five poems previously printed in *The New Age*), for which Pound wrote a prefatory note introducing *Les Imagistes* as the

---

[1] The tea-shop locale is mentioned by Aldington, *Life for Life's Sake* (New York, 1941). Pound simply says that Imagism began in Church Walk.

[2] Quoted by Harriet Monroe, *A Poet's Life* (New York, 1938), 259.

descendants of a "forgotten school of 1909," organized by Hulme.

He has come to regret his allusion to Hulme. Imagist doctrine seemed, at least implicitly, to bear a strong resemblance to certain of Hulme's theories. Pound was certainly acquainted with the "forgotten school," and, since the publication of F. S. Flint's "History of Imagism" in 1915, there has been rather wide agreement that credit for Imagist theory belongs to Hulme and that Pound merits only the dubious honor of publicizing another man's ideas—and there is some evidence to support this belief. Hulme organized his first poetry club in 1908, but when it began to develop along lines of excessive social formality and poetic conservatism, he resigned, and, with Flint, assembled another, more congenial group, whose weekly meetings date from March of 1909. The interests of this club were more radical: assuming a need for experiment, the members studied other literatures—the Japanese and Hebrew poets and the French Symbolists—for techniques that might benefit English poetry, giving special attention to the use of imagery and the ways of achieving an exact and efficient diction. Pound was present at some of those meetings, and his own remarks testify to the pleasure with which he recalled them at a later date, but he was mainly preoccupied with a study of the troubadour poets and Flint says that discussions of poetry interested him only when they could be illustrated or refuted by examples from troubadour verse.

Although the 1909 club lasted only a year, it was followed by the brilliant Frith Street evenings, which made Hulme better known among his contemporaries. While the poetry clubs were restricted in size and met in crowded Soho restaurants, these evenings drew a large number of guests and were held in a spacious home. As one writer recalls them, they were attended by "journalists, writers, poets, painters, politicians of all sorts, from Conservatives to New Age Socialists, Fabians, Irish Yaps, American bums, and Labour leaders."[3] Conversation obviously would not have been limited to poetry, although many poets, including Pound, Aldington, and Flint were present from time to time.

By 1912, the evenings had brought Hulme a prominence which certainly gave Pound one reason for including "The Complete Poetical Works" at the close of his own volume. His prefatory note, however, phrased the reference to Hulme's 1909 club with more than a little ambiguity:

As for the "School of Images," which may or may not have existed, its principles were not so interesting as those of the "inherent dynamists" or of *Les Unanimistes*, yet they were probably sounder than those of a certain French school which attempted to dispense with verbs altogether; or of the Impressionists who brought forth:

"Pink pigs blossoming upon the hillside";

or of the Post Impressionists who beseech their ladies to let down slate-blue hair over their raspberry-coloured flanks. . . .

As for the future, *Les Imagistes*, the descendants of the forgotten school of 1909, have that in their keeping.

I refrain from publishing my proposed *Historical Memoir* of their forerunners, because Mr. Hulme has threatened to print the original propaganda.[4]

It is not inevitable that Pound should have absorbed

[3] C. R. W. Nevinson, *Paint and Prejudice* (London, 1937), 63.
[4] *Ripostes* (London, 1912), 58.

Imagist doctrine from Hulme's theorizing at the 1909 club or the Frith Street evenings, even though both undoubtedly owed a large measure of their success to Hulme's powers as a conversationalist. In the first place, Pound has said that the conversations about poetry were conducted on the philosophical level which interested Hulme rather than on the level of the practicing poet, who found it necessary to supplement them with discussions of poetry carried on elsewhere. Further, Hulme did not in any sense preside over the meetings, holding the floor for himself; the talk was never guided by one person, nor was there any attempt to address the gathering as a whole—one did not attend simply to hear Hulme discourse upon art and poetry.

Announcement of *Les Imagistes* in a volume whose circulation was as limited as *Ripostes'* was only a preliminary step, and Pound had already discovered possibilities for wider publicity through his association with *Poetry* magazine. The first number of *Poetry* was to appear the month after publication of *Ripostes*, with Pound as its foreign correspondent, a position he held officially for seven years. Although he would have preferred a magazine of his own, he was glad enough to accept this job, for it gave him control over European contributions to one magazine, and to a magazine which paid its contributors. For her part, Miss Monroe was more than pleased to have Pound on her editorial staff; she had confidence in his judgment and knew that he could obtain poems from men like Yeats and Tagore and from promising unknowns like Aldington and H. D.

As a favor to Pound, she wrote a note on Imagism for the November issue of *Poetry*. Taking a cue from *Ripostes*, she linked *Les Imagistes* with French verse, describing them as poets who tried to "attain in English certain subtleties

7

of cadence of the kind which Mallarmé and his followers have studied in French." In the same note she also described them as a group of "ardent Hellenists." Neither of these descriptions threw much light on the school's title, though they were not necessarily inconsistent with what Pound had said. Thus, when the January issue of *Poetry* printed H. D.'s first poems (signed—at Pound's request—"H. D. Imagiste"), poems which seemed to confirm the Hellenist label, Imagism emerged as a school with ambitious, if somewhat diverse, aims.

In addition to H. D.'s poems, the January issue carried some of Pound's comment.

The youngest school here that has the nerve to call itself a school is that of the *Imagistes*.

Space forbids me to set forth the program of the *Imagistes* at length, but one of their watchwords is Precision, and they are in opposition to the numerous and unassembled writers who busy themselves with dull and interminable effusions, and who seem to think that a man can write a good long poem before he learns to write a good short one, or even before he learns to produce a good single line.[5]

It is little wonder that *Poetry* began to receive requests for more information about the school; readers could make little of the Symbolist-Hellenist-Precisionist combination, but Pound kept them waiting two more months before announcing his program more specifically. In March, 1913, he offered his "A Few Don'ts by an Imagiste" and Flint's "Imagisme," which was a discussion of the school's aims. Although Flint had met with them frequently, he was not

[5] "Status Rerum," *Poetry*, Vol. 1, No. 4 (January, 1913), 126.

yet one of the Imagists and was not inclined to take the movement seriously, but his article purported to be objective comment by a friendly but disinterested observer. He reported that their principles were mainly these:

1. Direct treatment of the "thing," whether subjective or objective.
2. To use absolutely no word that did not contribute to the presentation.
3. As regarding rhythm: to compose in sequence of the musical phrase, not in sequence of a metronome.[6]

He also alluded to a doctrine of the Image, which he said the Imagists preferred not to discuss, and which Pound's article clarified only to a certain extent.

"A Few Don'ts" (first intended as a rejection slip for *Poetry*) consisted of recommendations for the inexperienced poet, especially on ways in which he might improve his ear. It began by defining the Image:

An "Image" is that which presents an intellectual and emotional complex in an instant of time. I use the term "complex" rather in the technical sense employed by the newer psychologists, such as Hart, though we might not agree absolutely in our application.

It is the presentation of such a "complex" instantaneously which gives that sense of sudden liberation; that sense of freedom from time limits and space limits; that sense of sudden growth, which we experience in the presence of the greatest works of art.

[6] "Imagism," *Poetry*, Vol. I, No. 6 (March, 1913), 199.

It is better to present one Image in a lifetime than to produce voluminous works.[7]

This was followed by brief comments on its use, demanding concreteness and warning sternly against the danger of abstractions, but it provided no clearer statement of exactly what set *Imagistes* apart from others interested in sound poetic practice.

Pound was indebted to Harriet Monroe for the opportunity to give his school effective promotion, but neither he nor the other Imagists were ever entirely satisfied with the policies of her magazine. He had not been foreign correspondent for a year when he began to feel that *Poetry* was complacently ignoring the need for a continuous educational campaign that would lead to the "American *Risorgimento.*"[8] Specifically, he objected to the implications of the masthead motto, "To have great poets there must be great audiences too." He wanted the campaign directed to the few who were capable of reading and writing poetry, not to the masses, for whom poetry was not intended. He also disliked what he considered Miss Monroe's insufficiently critical enthusiasm for poets of Chicago and the Midwest, her inclination to accept poems on a basis not exclusively literary. In his letters he was most explicit about her tendency to "Christianize" his poems, on one occasion warning her not to "brandish the blue pencil of decency until you have weighed the outrages against the undercurrent of hygiene." Later, he wrote: "Cut out any of my poems that would be likely to get you suppressed but don't make it into a flabby little Sunday School lot."

[7] "A Few Don'ts by an Imagiste," *Poetry*, Vol. I, No. 6 (March, 1913), 200–201.
[8] Quoted by Monroe, *A Poet's Life*, 259.

The objections of the other Imagists were similar to Pound's. John Gould Fletcher accused Miss Monroe of desiring "to uphold Chicago and the Middle West at all hazards."[9] He urged her to establish a list of permanent contributors, to give up the damaging effort to publish too many new poets, and even offered to guarantee financial assistance if she would agree to his proposals. William Carlos Williams also encountered the blue pencil of decency and recommended a "little less pure beauty and a little roughness of contour added." Williams and Flint, as well as Pound, had difficulty with her over such matters as line arrangement, paragraph indentation, and initial capitals. To complicate the situation, feeling grew among Aldington, H. D., and Amy Lowell that Miss Monroe too often listened to Pound's advice and would publish his work but not theirs. The truth was that *Poetry*, in spite of its services to Imagism, would never become an Imagist magazine. Although it eventually printed poems by all the Imagists, its pages were open to any poet who seemed to show promise, and particularly, as the Imagists well knew, to poets who wrote what Miss Monroe felt best expressed the spirit of her own country.

As a result of *Poetry's* campaign, however, other little magazines took notice of the movement. Harold Monro's *Poetry and Drama* published a respectful summary of each of the *Poetry* articles, describing Imagism as "a new school of English poetry, still at present very small, and under the formidable dictatorship of Ezra Pound."[10] Rebecca West reported in *The New Freewoman* that the Imagists were efficient craftsmen, and, like Monro, said that their guiding

[9] *Life Is My Song* (New York, 1937), 192.
[10] "The Imagistes," *Poetry and Drama*, Vol. I, No. 2 (June, 1913), 127.

principle was that the poet should write in accordance with the best tradition. What they needed now was a magazine of their own, one in which they could formulate their own editorial policy and concentrate upon measures which would bring them wider recognition. The movement had begun only half-seriously, and no doubt Flint was surprised, as he wrote, to see Pound acting as if he had invented a wholly new aesthetic; but it had, with *Poetry's* help, progressed to the point where it was taken seriously in some quarters at least.

The Imagists finally found their magazine in *The New Freewoman*. Managed by Harriet Shaw Weaver and Dora Marsden, *The New Freewoman* was devoted primarily to learned articles by Miss Marsden on Bergson, radical feminism, and other more or less allied subjects. There was some difficulty in filling the remaining pages, and Pound persuaded the women that what their magazine needed was a well-edited literary section. They were unable to pay its contributors, but this proved to be no problem, for he soon met John Gould Fletcher, who was looking for some way he could use part of his income to help young, unpublished writers. In August, 1913, Pound wrote Harriet Monroe that he had taken charge of the magazine's literary pages; the next year, in order to suggest its new range of interest, *The New Freewoman* became *The Egoist*, which at least eliminated the emphasis upon militant feminism. Pound did not himself become officially connected with *The Egoist*, but from December, 1913, until 1917, Aldington was its assistant editor, and he was succeeded by another of Pound's discoveries, T. S. Eliot. The continuity of his influence was not as unbroken as this would suggest, for Aldington and Eliot developed authority in their own right with the editors; but, regardless of the particular person in power at any moment, the Imagists now had an assured outlet for their writing.

And by this time Pound could do even more for them. He "knew almost everyone worth knowing, and scarcely an American poet passed through London but found his way to Ezra's flat."[11] This was partially what he had been working toward ever since his arrival in London. He had begun by making himself known to Yeats, whom he considered the greatest living poet, and he soon came to dominate the colorful gathering which assembled at Yeats' flat for his Monday "evenings." Yeats had great faith in Pound's critical faculty, once submitting to him all of his verse for criticism, especially of passages containing too much abstraction. He did not, of course, give him absolute editorial authority, and he was not, even by 1913, prepared to say exactly what poetic contribution he expected Pound to make, but there is no question that he considered him a promising talent. On his side, Pound profited by the relationship: there was the prestige he could command with editors to whom he could promise a poem or two by Yeats, and, more important, the encouragement Yeats gave him in his own work—he wrote to William Carlos Williams in 1909: "I have been praised by the greatest living poet. I am after eight years hammering against impenetrable adamant suddenly become somewhat of a success."

He had been quick to make friends with another influential literary figure, Ford Madox Hueffer, who in December, 1908, brought out the first number of *The English Review*. Although Hueffer remained as editor for only fifteen months, the magazine's literary reputation was firm-

[11] John Cournos, *Autobiography* (New York, n.d.), 271.

ly established when he left; a writer for *The New Age* said that he "managed to publish more genuine literature than was ever . . . got into fifteen numbers of a monthly review before."[12] To him goes the credit for discovering D. H. Lawrence and for publishing Pound and Wyndham Lewis when they had not yet won any appreciable recognition. His associates had been mainly men like Hardy and Conrad, but he devoted more and more of his time and attention to *les jeunes,* and it was they who dominated the group which met afternoons as his guests at South Lodge. As at Yeats' evenings, the central figure was Pound, who conducted the assembly through a routine of tennis, followed by discussion of *vers libre,* the prosody of Arnaut Daniel, and " 'the villainy of contributors to the front page of the *Times Literary Supplement.*' "[13] The relationship with Hueffer gave Pound an impressive magazine outlet for his own writing, and the benefit of what he considered astute critical guidance.

In these years between 1908 and 1913, Pound made other valuable acquaintances. He was invited to the periodic "evenings" held by Ernest Rhys, who hoped to carry the spirit of the Rhymer's Club into the new century; he attended meetings of the Poetry Club, a conservative organization presided over by Sir Henry Newbolt. (Of Newbolt and certain of his associates, Pound has argued that they "at any rate WROTE something now and again, and however much one disagreed with 'em, one was at least disagreeing with something.") At Hulme's evenings he met A. R. Orage, whose *New Age* literary columns after 1912 began to pub-

[12] Jacob Tonson [Arnold Bennett], "Books and Persons," *The New Age,* Vol. VI, No. 13 (January 27, 1910), 305.

[13] Douglas Goldring, *South Lodge* (London, 1943), 47. Goldring is here quoting Hueffer.

lish some of his articles; and his friendship with Harold
Monro was particularly rewarding: both *The Poetry Review* and *Poetry and Drama* carried Imagist writing; and
the Poetry Bookshop, opened in 1912, not only sold volumes
not handled by most bookstores, but operated a press for
the publication of verse.

Pound used his contacts efficiently to assure publication
of creditable work from the many manuscripts which came
to him, and even to provide outright financial assistance
where necessary. When Fletcher was discouraged over his
failure to gain recognition, he introduced him to his friends,
and then, after mercilessly criticizing the "Irradiations"
to eliminate expressions he considered too obvious, sent the
revised manuscript to Harriet Monroe. Skipwith Cannell
also benefited from his generosity. He had come abroad on
a small allowance, the continuation of which depended on
his showing some success as a writer. After reading his
poems, Pound decided he was an artist, sent some of them
to W. H. Wright's *Smart Set,* and reserved part of a future
issue of *Poetry* for him. He introduced English readers
to the poetry of another American, William Carlos Williams. In October of 1912, Monro devoted *The Poetry Review* to modern American poetry, giving Pound an opportunity to present a selection of Williams' verse; this he
followed up by arranging with Elkin Mathews for publication of the complete manuscript from which the selections
had been taken.

Pound's ways and means of helping writers seemed almost limitless. As a reviewer, he promoted *les jeunes* wher-
ever possible. He saw Allen Upward's "Scented Leaves" in
Poetry, and was so impressed that he arranged to have a
selection from them published in *The New Freewoman;*

when Upward's prose volume, *The Divine Mystery,* appeared, Pound reviewed it with vigorous, unqualified approval. Having helped Lawrence to publication in *The English Review* after Hueffer had been forced out, he announced *Love Poems and Others* as "the most important book of poems of the season."[14] Privately he expressed a less favorable personal reaction and, by 1915, he was not so enthusiastic about Lawrence's "loaded, ornate style, heavy with sex, fruity with a certain sort of emotion";[15] but his earlier praise helped bring him into the Imagist circle. Lawrence's comment is interesting: "The Hueffer-Pound faction seems inclined to lead me around a little as one of their show dogs. They seem to have a certain ear in their possession. If they are inclined to speak my name into the ear, I don't care."[16]

Finally, Amy Lowell entered the Pound sphere of influence. She first visited London in the summer of 1913, with a letter of introduction to him from Harriet Monroe; after some correspondence, he went to visit her and they spent a "most delightful evening" which "ended in his taking one of my poems to print in a group of 'Imagistes' in ... 'The New Freewoman,' and in his asking me to send another to the 'English Review.'" He introduced her to the other Imagists, Aldington, H. D., and Flint, who were soon teaching her Imagist principles and applying them to her verse, eliminating clichés and too obviously stated morals. Their criticism was painstaking and thorough—Pound said

[14] "In Metre," *The New Freewoman,* Vol. I, No. 6 (September 1, 1913), 113.
[15] "Affirmations," *The New Age,* Vol. XVI, No. 17 (February 25, 1915), 452.
[16] *The Letters of D. H. Lawrence,* ed. by Aldous Huxley (New York, 1932), 174.

to Robert Frost: "When I get through with that girl she'll think she was born in free verse,"[17] and toward the end of the summer, he had decided that "Miss Lowell is ALL RIGHT." She kept in touch with the Imagists upon her return to the United States: Pound for a time tried to persuade her to back a literary magazine, offering her the editorship of *The Egoist;* then he suggested that she finance a quarterly with Hueffer, Joyce, Lawrence, Flint, and himself as English editors and Miss Lowell and her choice of contributors as American. While she did not accept either of the proposals, she sent him money to distribute as he saw fit; she was convinced of Imagism's importance, and, against Fletcher's advice, had evidently decided that she should identify herself more closely with this program for a new poetry.

Pound's next move in publicizing his school was to enlarge its representation. As a preliminary measure, he arranged publication in *The New Freewoman* for September, 1913, of a group of poems by "the Newer School." Since the group included verse by the Imagists, Aldington and H. D., and by Flint, whose name was associated with the Imagists, the "school" was clearly Imagism; and since their verse appeared here alongside that of Cannell, Williams, and Amy Lowell, Imagism had clearly admitted some new members. At the same time, he was planning similar but more impressive steps: in September, he wrote to Miss Lowell, asking her if she would be willing to contribute to an Imagist anthology. The effectiveness of anthology publication had been demonstrated in 1912 by Edward Marsh's *Georgian Anthology,* which had been an immediate success, its sales running to around 15,000 copies. Pound had little

[17] Quoted by Monroe, *A Poet's Life,* 275.

use for the Wordsworthianism of the Georgians, but he could learn from their experience, and he may have intended that Imagism become a counterblast to the poetry of a school receiving wider recognition than he felt it deserved.

At any rate, he began inviting poets to contribute to an anthology of verse by *Les Imagistes,* and set about to find a publisher. Harold Monro, whose Bookshop press had published the Georgian anthology, agreed to handle the English edition of Pound's volume. Finding an American publisher was more difficult, but John Cournos, another American who owed his start in London to Pound, knew of one. Alfred Kreymborg had written him asking for contributions to his magazine, *The Glebe,* and he passed the request along to Pound, who forwarded the manuscript of poems by his *Imagistes.* Kreymborg was unable to publish it immediately, for his press broke down and he had to find someone to pay for repairs, but the proprietors of the Washington Square Bookshop came to his aid, and the February, 1914, issue of *The Glebe* was devoted to *Des Imagistes: An Anthology.* It contained nine poems by Aldington, seven by H. D., six by Pound, five by Flint, and one each by Hueffer, Williams, Cannell, Lowell, Upward, Cournos, and James Joyce (who, as his biographer has pointed out, was also indebted to Pound for help during these years).

Almost immediately after the publication of *Des Imagistes* in 1914, Pound's interest in the Imagist poets began to waver and he turned his energy to another movement, this time not in poetry but in painting. He made friends among painters and sculptors because "one's *contemporaries* in the full sense of the term, are nearly always artists who use some other medium." One of them was Percy Wyndham Lewis whom he met in 1910 and of whom he later wrote in *The Egoist:* "Mr. Lewis has got into his work something which I recognize as the voice of my own age,"[18] at the time the highest praise he could give. Another was the sculptor Henri Gaudier-Brzeska, whom he was able to help by finding buyers for his work.

Among the artists, a principal subject of current interest was a movement called Futurism. One of its aims was overthrow of the traditional and academic in art, and on this ground it was acceptable, though its continental origins and blatantly eccentric and sensational propaganda were less attractive. Those who felt that some sort of revolution was necessary, but who disapproved the form it was taking in Futurism, set up a native movement in opposition: Lewis, Gaudier, Hulme, and others first opposed Futurism by harassing its meetings; then Lewis organized what became known as Vorticism, with a combination meeting place and school called the Rebel Art Centre.

Pound threw his energy and organizational ability into the movement, and Vorticism assumed a responsibility for poetry as well as for the other arts. The Centre was to branch out into instruction in all the arts, with Pound and Hueffer lecturing on literature. The Vorticists also decided to hire a theater for a series of performances (readings and lectures) which would inform the public of their aims. But there was no rush of applicants for the Centre course, and the plan to hire the theater fell through. One idea did materialize, however: the Vorticists succeeded in bringing out a magazine appropriately called *Blast.*

Blast was an experiment which did the movement, and Pound, a great deal of harm. At an inaugural tea party, the

18 "Wyndham Lewis," *The Egoist,* Vol. II, No. 8 (April 15, 1914), 234.

Vorticists decided upon their editorial policy and drew up a list of people to be blasted and a list of those to be blessed. The first of two issues appeared in June, 1914. It contained, in addition to its blasts (Bergson, Tagore, and others) and blessings (English humor, French pornography and females, Joyce, and so on), a manifesto signed by eleven men, including Aldington, Gaudier, Pound, and Lewis. Pound contributed some of his poems, including "Salutation the Third," which attacked not only *TLS* reviewers but all who would turn art to commercial ends. Though extreme even for *Blast*, "Salutation the Third" suggests something of the tone of the magazine. The language of the poem is abusive—more so as originally printed than as it appears in *Personae*—and its intemperate attitude and crude expression (even if meant to be amusing) are no credit to the author. While the reader, especially after thirty-five years, can see it in some perspective, he is not surprised to find Violet Hunt recalling that a woman to whom she sold a copy of *Blast* returned it because she was afraid her daughters might come upon it. In spite of the fact that the magazine and its later companion issue could boast a first short story by Rebecca West, poems by T. S. Eliot, cuts by Epstein and others, its tone was violent, aggressive, and, on occasion, in bad taste. It was perhaps just as well that the opening of the war with Germany brought the movement and its magazine to an end.

Pound did not completely lose his interest in Imagism. Although by the spring of 1914 he spoke of the Vortex instead of the Image, he tried to make the two synonymous by asserting the application of the Vortex to all the arts. His associations, however, were mainly with painters and sculptors, not poets, and with a movement that provoked a good deal of unfavorable criticism. It seemed that Vorticism would draw him aside from his original movement, which perhaps would be left to languish and disappear. What actually took place was that Pound was left high and dry when his movement was taken over by a woman who was at least as purposeful as he was and whose energy gave it a reputation which Pound had not been able to approach. He did not lose interest in Imagism; Imagism lost interest in him.

When Amy Lowell arrived in London for her second visit, Vorticism was in its early and most exuberant stages and Imagism was almost completely inarticulate. She wrote in July, 1914:

I find our little group more or less disintegrated and broken up. Violent jealousy has broken out, whether because of the "Imagiste Anthology" and its reviews, I cannot say. Poor old Ezra has got himself into a most silly movement of which "Blast" is the organ. . . . My feeling is that his slanging of the public, and his indecent poems, have flattened out his reputation, even Hueffer tells me that Ezra is very unhappy because he is so unsuccessful. The opinion of everyone is that he has nothing more to say. . . . The craze for advertisement has swept Ezra off his feet. His Imagiste movement is petering out because of the lack of vigor in his poets, and the complete indifference of the public. . . . It seems now as though it were simply a flair of young men with nothing more in them.

As soon as Miss Lowell arrived in London, Pound again brought up the matter of an international review which they had discussed in correspondence during the preceding year.[19]

[19] My account of the Pound-Lowell break is based largely upon the detailed report of it which Miss Lowell wrote to Miss Monroe. S. Foster Damon, *Amy Lowell* (Boston & New York, 1935), 237–39, has quoted most of the letter, which is dated September 15, 1914.

Now his terms were that she should provide $5,000 annually, which they agreed was the minimum for financing such a magazine, and contribute whatever number of poems she wished; he was to be salaried editor. Her reply that she could not afford so large a sum angered him, and he accused her of unwillingness to bestow her money on the arts. She persisted in her refusal, but began to consider an alternative which would be more suitable to her means and still provide help for at least a few writers: republishing the Imagist anthology with the same contributors each year for five years as a way of establishing the movement and its members; "by constant iteration to make some impression upon the reading public," as the Georgians were doing.

She mentioned her plan first to the Aldingtons "because I saw them first after I conceived the idea," and added certain of her own suggestions as to how the new anthology should be edited: she wanted it to be democratic, with each poet allowed the same space, and she wanted a publisher of reputable standing, which she would get even if she had to pay the costs of publication herself. The Aldingtons were enthusiastic, as were others whom she asked to join; but Pound's reaction was to accuse her of trying to make herself editor. He refused to go along with the new anthology unless she would provide $200 a year for some indigent poet. The request was not tactfully stated; Miss Lowell felt that he was attempting to intimidate her, and though she was willing to help anyone who needed it, she did not wish to be forced into an agreement. Again she rejected his terms.

Pound was fighting a losing battle. He mistakenly forced the issue by asking the Aldingtons to choose between him and Miss Lowell and finally by asking them to join him in an anthology which would exclude her. Despite the fact that they were deeply indebted to him and the decision was difficult, they considered Miss Lowell's plan fair and believed that they should accept it, if only on principle. Flint, Lawrence, and Hueffer joined the discussions and

we all agreed that Ezra could not expect to run us all his own way forever, and that if he chose to separate himself from us, we should be obliged, although most regretfully, to let him.

The group approved the plan for the new anthologies and left Pound outside the movement he had begun.

There is little reason to question the authenticity of Miss Lowell's version of the disagreement. Perhaps the idea of promoting the series was already in her mind when she reached London; she had thought of financing *Des Imagistes*, and Damon says that her single-poem quota in that volume had wounded her pride because it made her appear to be only one of six poets included as padding. Pound's comments on the quarrel agree in general with Miss Lowell's: he objected mainly and strenuously to her idea of an editorial committee for the selection of anthology poems ("if I give way to, or saddle myself with, a dam'd contentious, probably incompetent committee . . . . If I tacitly . . . accept a certain number of people as my critical and creative equals, and publish the acceptance, I don't see the use. Moreover I should like the name 'Imagisme' to retain some sort of a meaning.") A demoralized committee would have turned Imagism into a "democratic beer-garden"; it could not be trusted to keep the hard light and clear edges.

Pound requested that certain steps be taken to formalize his secession from Imagism. "If anyone wants a faction . . . I think it can be done amicably, but I should think it wiser to split over an aesthetic principle" than over personal differences. The split over principle would require that the Lowell group find a new name. While Pound felt that he might sanction an Imagist anthology if it was clearly stated at the front of the book that he dissociated himself from responsibility for the contents and for any views of the contributors, still he was reluctant to give up his "machinery for gathering stray good poems . . . and of discovering new talent." He suggested as an alternative that the new anthologies be called *Vers Libre*, or something similar (though he would not protest use of *Imagisme* somewhere in a subtitle), and agreed that he would not publish a rival anthology in America before 1916.

He and Miss Lowell remained on terms of distant friendliness. With his wife he attended the Imagist dinner which she gave soon after her arrival, and they dined with her before she left; he underlined his attitude in a letter to Margaret Anderson: "Is there any life into which the personal Amy would not bring rays of sunshine?"[20] Miss Lowell forecast a break with Pound in a good-natured poem, "Astigmatism," dedicated to him, "With Much Friendship and Admiration and Some Differences of Opinion." After their clash, however, her feeling changed to resentment, and Pound had to chide her for describing their relationship as one of bitterest enmity.

The other Imagists expressed unreserved satisfaction over his refusal to join them and even wished to avoid using the name he had given the movement. Fletcher wrote:

I am very glad to hear this news and don't think you will lose much—if anything—by not having his contribution. . . .

[20] Quoted in *My Thirty Years' War* (New York, 1930), 164.

"Couldn't we call ourselves the Independents or the Vitalists or the young America group or something like that and dissasociate [*sic*] ourselves from any -isms except free verse and definite treatment of subject?"

Aldington was coming to regret his relationship with Pound and the Vorticists, whose erratic and violent behavior he thought bordered almost upon madness. As for Pound's exclusion from Imagism, it would not, he predicted, cripple the movement artistically, and in every other way seemed to him a distinct blessing. H. D. wrote an almost frantic request to Miss Lowell in December, 1914, that they drop Imagism from any title they might use; there was no doubt in their minds that the future of the movement lay along lines different from those Pound was pursuing.

II

The Imagist Movement, 1914-17

IMAGISM developed along divergent lines from 1914 to 1917: Pound continued to proclaim the Image, but it was Amy Lowell and her group who put before the public the doctrine by which the movement was most generally known. Although Harold Monro warned her that withdrawal of Pound's name would mean the collapse of Imagism, she soon proved that it no longer needed him.

Miss Lowell's first problem was the publication of the anthologies, which brought more trouble with Pound. In *Poetry* for September, 1914, Macmillan, announcing *Sword Blades and Poppy Seeds,* had described its author as "the foremost member of the 'Imagists'—a group of poets that includes William Butler Yeats, Ezra Pound, Ford Madox Hueffer . . . ." Pound saw the advertisement and expressed a rather mild reaction in a letter to Harriet Monroe, though he did suggest that were the publisher producing a commercial product, he would be open to suit for libel. A week later, however, he sent Miss Lowell a withering letter of protest strongly denouncing the publishers, and warning: "I think you had better cease referring to yourself as an Imagiste." He again hinted a libel suit, but she answered with equal vigor, daring him to sue.

Macmillan had also agreed to publish the proposed anthologies. Pound, however, wrote them regarding use of the Imagist name, and Miss Lowell had to look for another publisher. He continued his attack by writing an indignant article on publishers in general, which he tried to present through *The Egoist,* but Aldington intercepted it and forced Miss Weaver to suppress it by threatening resignation. Pound's reply was to announce that he was forwarding it to Macmillan directly, but he apparently did not do so.

Houghton Mifflin now agreed to bring out the anthologies for a three-year period, but there remained the question of the Imagist title. One publisher had been afraid of it, and the London poets were not enthusiastic about the continued association in print with Pound—in fact, by early 1915 they were on the point of dropping the anthology itself. Miss Lowell, however, insisted upon *Imagism* or *Imagist,* for the word had already a certain authority, and, when Pound suggested as a compromise that she call her book *Some Imagist Poets* (thus avoiding the implication that the anthologies included all the Imagists and, by dropping the *e,* marking a distinction between her school and his), she was able to secure the approval of the London group. The problem solved, the Imagists enthusiastically resumed their plans:

The change of title will rid us of Ezra, and after that "Pride's Purge" the remaining band of us, loyal, open and disinterested, as I believe we are, should not only make a stir in the world but, what is more important, produce work of first-rate quality.[1]

The first *Some Imagist Poets* appeared in 1915. Origi-

[1] Aldington, letter (unpublished) to Amy Lowell, December 7, 1914.

nally there were to have been seven contributors: Aldington, H. D., Flint, Amy Lowell, Fletcher, D. H. Lawrence (who was to take Pound's place), and Hueffer, but the list was reduced to six when the publishers would not accept Hueffer's contribution, a long and highly regarded poem entitled "On Heaven," which placed Heaven somewhere near Lyons in southern France. The volume contained a long preface which acknowledged a debt to Ezra Pound without mentioning his name and went on to state a poetic doctrine representing the areas which the six contributors agreed to be common ground. The principles, which will be considered in more detail in Chapter VII, were these:

1. To use the language of common speech, but to employ always the *exact* word, not the nearly-exact, nor the merely decorative word.

2. To create new rhythms—as the expression of new moods—and not to copy old rhythms, which merely echo old moods. We do not insist upon "free-verse" as the only method of writing poetry. We fight for it as for a principle of liberty. We believe that the individuality of a poet may often be better expressed in free-verse than in conventional forms. In poetry, a new cadence means a new idea.

3. To allow absolute freedom in the choice of subject. It is not good art to write badly about aeroplanes and automobiles; nor is it necessarily bad art to write well about the past. We believe passionately in the artistic value of modern life, but we wish to point out that there is nothing so uninspiring nor so old-fashioned as an aeroplane of the year 1911.

4. To present an image (hence the name: "Imagist"). We are not a school of painters, but we believe that poetry should render

28

particulars exactly and not deal in vague generalities, however magnificent and sonorous. It is for this reason that we oppose the cosmic poet, who seems to us to shirk the real difficulties of his art.

5. To produce poetry that is hard and clear, never blurred nor indefinite.

6. Finally, most of us believe that concentration is of the very essence of poetry.

In America, *Some Imagist Poets* (1915) had an immediately successful sale which reached 1,301 copies the first year;[2] in England, where it was published by Constable, it got off to a slower start: the sheets for publication were late in arriving and thus missed the opportunity for a good sale created by interest in *The Egoist's* "Imagist Number." But in a few months the situation looked more encouraging; Aldington wrote to Miss Lowell:

I enclose a few press-cuttings. It is interesting to see that we are getting more reviews for this anthology than for the first. Also, as you will see, opinion is beginning slightly to turn our way. The next anthology, if we can keep up to the mark, ought to turn the scale.

It is necessary to speak only briefly of the two succeeding volumes. There was some discussion of introducing new names into the movement. Aldington, for example, suggested that the 1916 anthology might include Williams, John Cournos, Allen Upward, and Marianne Moore (whom he "discovered" in *The Egoist*), his idea being to extend Imagism's too narrow limits. Fletcher wanted to

[2] Damon, *Amy Lowell*, 368.

lure from Pound's circle T. S. Eliot, whom he considered "the only fresh *possibility* that I see in present-day poetry." There was also some difficulty with at least one of the incumbents. Miss Lowell was hesitant about continuing the association with D. H. Lawrence because of the accusations of obscenity being made against him; Aldington was able to overcome her doubts on this score, though it is clear that Lawrence was an Imagist only by courtesy of the others: "we only included him from sympathy and to try and educate him."[3] But the 1916 *Some Imagist Poets* emerged from the democratic editorial process with the same six contributors, and its sale kept up with the first; by September 30 it had gone into a third American edition.

For 1917, H. D. had to handle the editorial duties for the London Imagists as Aldington was in military service. There was still some question about Lawrence, this time from his side. He apparently had been rather apathetic toward Imagist aims and enthusiasms, but he was badly in need of the financial assistance which Miss Lowell was able to provide, and his gratitude for her generous help kept him within the circle. There was little talk now of adding to the movement; Fletcher even began to express doubts about continuing the volumes—he was not sympathetic to the very general doctrine which the group had published in its preface-manifestoes, and he did not think the work of all the contributors worth the effort and money Miss Lowell was spending. She announced after the 1917 anthology:

[3] "This (I sincerely hope) was meant as a joke. In case anyone takes it seriously, let me state my mature conviction that Lawrence's poetry is immeasureably superior to mine."—Richard Aldington, in a letter to the author, May 16, 1950.

There will be no more volumes of "Some Imagist Poets." The collection has done its work. These little books are the germ, the nucleus, of the school; its spreading out, its amplification, must be sought in the published work of the individual members of the group.[4]

The others conceded the wisdom of her decision; H. D. wrote:

I think we all feel the same about the Anthology. It was splendid for the three years—but its work, as you say, is finished—its collective work that is. Each of us has gained by the brother-ship but we are all developing along different lines—all of us who are developing.

The anthologies, testifying for the first time to the existence of a specific body of Imagist doctrine as well as to a group of at least six members whose work attempted to illustrate the doctrine, were made possible by the tactful, yet capable and efficient, leadership of Miss Lowell. Her personality equipped her to deal with temperamental young poets, and, in an emergency, she could add the authority of an influential name and a comfortable income. While the Imagists themselves were probably not impressed by her name and could not be said to have been won by her money, they were aware of the prestige of both, especially in America. She was a strong central figure to whom the others could turn for assistance.

There is no doubt about her tact. The Macmillan advertisement which provoked Pound to violent language did not go unnoticed among her own group; there was some

[4] *Tendencies in Modern American Poetry* (Boston, 1931), 255.

objection to the inclusion of Hueffer's and Yeats' names, and Flint frankly resented Macmillan's omission from their list of any of the group who were to be in the 1915 anthology. Upon seeing the advertisement, Miss Lowell immediately sent Aldington a wire of apology, which, while it did not put a full stop to the grumbling, helped smooth ruffled feelings. Again, when Harriet Monroe referred to her in *Poetry* as editor of *Some Imagist Poets*, Miss Lowell hastened to set her straight on the fact that the anthologies had no editor: "These poets are touchy people, and not for a moment would I have them think that I arrogated to myself a position which was not mine."

Fletcher's admiration for her required the exercise of further tact. On one occasion, he wrote an article for *The Egoist* in which he described her as the foremost Imagist and, comparing her work to Shakespeare's, predicted that she would take her place among the masters. Aldington, Flint, H. D., and Monro, working together, went over his article, carefully purging it of all references which they considered overenthusiastic. It was all done, as Aldington later wrote to Miss Lowell, "with the best of intentions," and there was no apparent resentment, though Flint referred to Fletcher's Shakespeare-Lowell comparison in the course of a letter to her. It is clear that there would be no "foremost" Imagist in a democratic movement and that she was wise in her conscientious efforts to be tactful.

That she was a good business woman and on occasion was able to provide extra money also helped her keep the group together. She managed the royalties from the anthologies, and the checks she forwarded to England were often large enough to cause some grateful comment. Her subscriptions to the Poets' Translation Series published by

The Egoist put the project in sound financial condition. At Aldington's request, she helped the French poet and critic, Remy de Gourmont, whose income was cut off by the war, by advancing him money and placing some of his work in America. When in late 1914 *The Egoist* seemed unable to continue, Aldington accepted a small sum from her, though he would not allow her to become its sole backer. She was eager, however, to buy her way into this magazine, and when she found that it was impossible for her to do so, she offered Aldington £100 for starting an independent review. He would not accept American patronage for an English magazine, but suggested the promotion of an Imagist review in the United States with himself as English editor. By the close of 1915 the idea had developed into an ambitious plan for an American *Mercure,* to which she had agreed to contribute $5,000. Aldington hoped to be able to get to the United States, but conscription put an end to the project.

Finally, she was a center of strength for the anthology poets because of her relationships with certain American journals and publishing houses. To *Poetry* she subscribed first $100 and later $200 yearly and saw to it that her publishers advertised liberally in the magazine. As a consequence she had some influence when she wished to place work by her friends, though she was far from having any control of editorial policy. In 1915 she tried to gain an editorial position elsewhere by offering to subsidize Margaret Anderson's *Little Review;* she was willing to contribute $150 a month to the impecunious magazine and allow Miss Anderson to retain control, provided she be permitted to direct the poetry department as she wished. Miss Anderson needed the money, but she refused to give an opening of any kind to the aggressive Miss Lowell. Some credit was also due her for raising money to found W. S. Braithwaite's *Poetry Review of America,* and she was able to get Aldington a position as London correspondent for this magazine. Her authority with publishers in America was far more commanding than Pound's had been: she persuaded Houghton Mifflin to publish Fletcher's *Irradiations,* as well as the anthologies.

Once reorganized and unified by Amy Lowell's leadership, the Imagists did not rest solely upon the anthologies to establish their position, but energetically sought other ways to make themselves and their work known to a wider public. Aldington contributed most effectively to advancing the cause in England. As assistant editor of *The Egoist,* he conceived and executed plans for an Imagist number which appeared on May 1, 1915, and helped create an audience for the first anthology. In addition to Flint's "History of Imagism" (designed to show the school's independence of Pound) and Harold Monro's shrewd comments on the forthcoming anthology, there were articles on the work of each of the Imagist poets (including Pound) and poems by the six members of Amy Lowell's group, as well as by Marianne Moore and May Sinclair. Pound had been asked to contribute a poem and to ask Williams for one, but he failed to answer, and when the Imagist number appeared, sent strong letters about it to Aldington and Flint. In England, the Imagist number sent the circulation of the magazine up by over two hundred, brought in new subscriptions, and stirred interest in the anthology, which was to reach the bookstores in June. It was less effective in the United States. Miss Lowell found a bookstore in New York and one in Boston which would take copies on a commission basis and asked Harriet Monroe to find a similar outlet in Chicago; but when she saw the issue, she regretted her efforts. She was afraid of American readers' reactions to Monro's honest but generally unfavorable criticism and to Lawrence's poem, which she considered indecent; in lieu of selling the magazine, she sent Miss Weaver a check for her commission on 150 *Egoists*.

Aldington used other methods to publicize the movement. He made one or two attempts to schedule lectures on Imagism in London, but the plans did not work out. He tried to make the movement known on the Continent: by corresponding with Remy de Gourmont in Paris and with other French poets, by distributing and encouraging the sale of their little magazines in England, he hoped to gain support and publicity for his own movement. The actual results in number of printed columns devoted to Imagism were not wholly satisfactory, but the *Mercure de France* gave its readers a brief notice of the English poets.

Amy Lowell's publicity was more aggressive. Before the 1915 anthology appeared, she decided to take her case before the organization likely to present the most effective opposition. The Poetry Society of America, with headquarters in New York City, had grown impressively since its founding in 1910. Extremely conservative, it nevertheless seemed to fill a need among poets for a place to gather and discuss their art, and attracted visitors representing widely varying views; when Pound returned to this country for a visit, he attended some meetings, but the Society inclined generally to a conservatism which held his Imagist movement up to scorn and ridicule. Amy Lowell in March, 1915, asked permission to appear before this formidable organization, and was given five minutes at the close of a meeting that featured the introduction of Masters' *Spoon River Anthology*. Her opening remarks summarized Imagist doctrine, and she followed with a reading of two of her own poems. A strictly observed Society rule demanded that there should be no criticism of poetry read by a guest, but that evening the rule was forgotten in the din of heated controversy over her poetry. In the forum which extended far beyond the originally alloted five minutes, she defended herself and her school so ably and provocatively that henceforth she became known to American readers as not only the leader but the founder of Imagism.

She helped organize her own New England Poetry Club and became its first president in order to offset the opposition from the Poetry Society of America. She met and corresponded with prominent reviewers and critics, arguing the case for her own kind of poetry. With both Louis Untermeyer and Professor J. L. Lowes, for example, she developed friendships which helped assure a fairer and more reasonable hearing for Imagism. She was careful to keep her movement clear of what she considered harmful associations, such as Kreymborg's "Others" group, though in this case she and Fletcher contributed to the *Others* anthology before they changed their minds and decided to withdraw: "we did not like their methods, and we did not want people to think that they were Imagists."[5] Perhaps most important, she carried the fight to a less professional public with her skillful and polished readings. As early as 1914 she could write proudly that four hundred people had heard her read "The Bombardment"; though this was in her home town of Brookline, by 1916 she was turning peo-

[5] Amy Lowell, letter (unpublished) to Harriet Monroe, January 26, 1916.

ple away from readings held in Chicago and other Western cities.

Yet, through 1917, unfavorable and unfriendly criticism predominated. *Poetry* almost alone among the magazines gave Imagism reasoned and unemotional consideration, and even its reviews tended to deprecate the loss in the *Some Imagist Poets* volumes of the hard, clear outline which had originally characterized Imagist doctrine and poetry. A brief glance at the opinions of a few prominent reviewers will serve to illustrate the general attitude. Conrad Aiken attacked the Imagists as "a very loud-voiced little mutual-admiration society" and objected to the lack of form and emotional force displayed in the poetry. O. W. Firkins published a less violent criticism of Imagist formlessness, again opposing their theories of *vers libre*. Padraic Colum criticized them as worse egoists than Byron, "who at least left mountains as big as he found them." And Lewis Worthington Smith, writing for the *Atlantic Monthly*, continued the attack by deriding them for "egotistic self-conscious ness." [6] The critics, in sum, objected mainly to the Imagist's concern with his own personal reactions, no matter how trivial, and to his use of a "formless" free verse. Perhaps the most withering remarks of all were those contained in a series of articles written by William Ellery Leonard for *The Chicago Evening Post* during September and October of 1915.

The strength and authority of the opposition testify at

[6] Aiken, "The Place of Imagism," *The New Republic*, Vol. III, No. 29 (May 22, 1915), 75-76; Firkins, "The New Movement in Poetry," *The Nation*, Vol. 101, No. 262 (October 14, 1915), 458-60; Colum, "Egoism in Poetry," *The New Republic*, Vol. V, No. 55 (November 2, 1915), 6-7; Smith, "The New Naïveté," *Atlantic Monthly*, Vol. CXVII, No. 4, (April, 1916), 487-92.

least to the fact that Imagism could no longer be safely or honestly ignored, and Amy Lowell asserted her right to a major share of credit for this:

The Imagists, during the year and a half in which he [Pound] headed the movement, were unknown and jeered at, when they were not absolutely ignored. It was not until I entered the arena, and Ezra dropped out, that Imagism began to be considered seriously at all. I feel sure that if I had not done all I did and worked seriously and hard to prove the value of the movement, the thing never would have achieved the recognition it now has. Ezra would have ruined it, important though it was. . . . The name is his, the idea was wide-spread, but changing over the whole public attitude from derision to consideration came from my work.

Her claim would seem to be justified: a glance at the names of the critics quoted above and of the magazines for which they wrote is adequate proof of the reputation Imagism had acquired, and it had established this reputation only after she had assumed leadership. Its fame had spread from the restricted circle of the little magazine into the broader area reached by the more popular journals. In the development, Pound's *Poetry* manifesto was forgotten, and Imagism became known as the poetry of the *Some Imagist Poets* volumes and the doctrine of their prefaces.

In the meantime, while Amy Lowell was so successfully exploiting his idea, Pound did not relax his efforts either for Imagism as he understood it or for modern poetry as he hoped to see it written. For a while, he continued to explain and publicize Imagism through the magazines to which he had access, writing articles on the subject for *Blast*, the *Fort-*

nightly Review, and *The New Age,* and relating the Image to the Vortex. Though the other poets had deserted him for Miss Lowell and though he had "no blood lust" over their desertion, he felt at first that "I must at least do what I can to keep *a* meaning for the word . . . ." And he did not feel that the Imagists had progressed as poets since their appearance in his anthology. Through an article for *Poetry,* which Miss Monroe toned down at Fletcher's suggestion, Pound publicly expressed his attitude toward his former colleagues: "The general weakness of the new school is looseness, lack of rhythmical construction and intensity,"[7] and in a later article:

Imagism, before it went off into froth, . . . had its first breath of air in these pages. At present its chief defects are sloppiness, lack of cohesion, lack of organic centre in individual poems, rhetoric, a conventional form of language to be found also in classical text-books, and in some cases a tendency more than slight towards the futurist's cinematographic fluidity.[8]

As a corrective he suggested to Harriet Monroe that she reprint his "Don'ts" with the addition of a few notes and emendations; he could thus make up an eight- or ten-page pamphlet to sell for ten cents, which should certainly pay its expenses.

It would be better than my writing new articles pointing out the various sorts of silliness into which neo-imagism or neogism is perambulating . . . ! The first anthology was designed to get

[7] "Correspondence," *Poetry,* Vol. VII, No. 6 (March, 1916), 323.
[8] "Status Rerum,—the Second," *Poetry,* Vol. VIII, No. 1 (April, 1916), 39.

printed and published the work of a few poets whose aim was to write a few excellent poems . . . rather than the usual magazine thousands of Elsa Barker, the futurist diarhoeaa [sic], rhetorical slush, etc. . . . I do not think the present methods of the neoists are in any way designed to further or foster the "few perfect" things against Chestertonian or Paul Fortian sloppiness.

Before long, however, he was willing to give up the movement: the *Dial* had printed an article which called T. S. Eliot an Imagist, and Pound wrote a vigorous reply which he sent to *Poetry:*

At the present moment there is no active united movement. There are a half dozen good newish poets innovating and renovating. . . . another firm has taken over the label as a trade asset, a firm consisting of people who aren't interested, who never were interested in the original tenets, or who, at the least, had never any intention of following them.[9]

For a time, when someone tried to take the Imagist name away from him, his temper had quickened his interest, but his restless mind soon turned to other ways of achieving Imagism's purpose.

The Rebel Art Centre school, planned as part of the Vorticist program, was one way of continuing the "educational campaign" in spite of the fact that Imagism was losing its usefulness. Its purpose was to "enable things to keep on here in spite of the war-strain and (what will be more dangerous) the war backwash and post-war slump."[10] Be-

[9] The article in typescript is to be found in the Harriet Monroe Collection.
[10] Quoted by Monroe, *A Poet's Life*, 355.

fore the scheme fell through, the organizers had issued a prospectus or preliminary announcement which proposed to interest the student of a single art, the serious general art students, and "the better sort of dilettante." The curriculum was intended to satisfy two assumptions:

A. That the arts INCLUDING poetry and literature should be taught by artists, by practicing artists NOT by sterile professors.

B. That the arts should be gathered together for the purpose of interenlightenment.

In 1915 he tried to carry the campaign to America, planning a manifesto to be signed by himself and Eliot and by Masters, Sandburg, Williams, and Johns; although its content is not known, he apparently made up a tentative statement and forwarded it to the poets for their signatures. His efforts went for nothing, however, for, as he said later, the others were not willing to sign without further discussion of the principles involved.

Another preoccupation was with the literature of China and Japan. His "Contemporania," published in *Poetry*, had at least one tangible result. Mrs. Ernest Fenollosa, widow of an American who had become imperial commissioner of arts in Japan, was at the time looking for someone to act as poet-interpreter for rendering into English poetry her husband's decipherings from the Chinese and Japanese. The "Contemporania" convinced her that Pound was the poet she sought and she forwarded to him her late husband's notes. As early as January, 1914, Pound admitted being literary executor for Fenollosa, though he did not want it known immediately. He was enthusiastic about his discovery: "Liu Ch'e, Chu Yuan, Chia I, and the great *vers libre* writers before the Petrarchan age of Li Po, are a treasure to which the next centuries may look for as great a stimulus as the Renaissance had from the Greeks."[11] In these literatures he saw a vitality and freshness which were a desirable stimulus to the revolution in the arts.

He continued his search for talented young poets. Among his discoveries after Aldington and H. D. were John Rodker and Iris Barry. He sent their work to *Poetry* and *The Little Review* and gave it a qualified approval: "I stake my critical position, or some part of it, on a belief that both of them *will* do something. . . . And one must have *les jeunes*."[12] But the culmination of his efforts to discover new poets took place late in 1914. He wrote Harriet Monroe in September: "An American called Eliot called this P.M. I think he has some sense tho' he has not yet sent me any verse."[13] Within a week he wrote her again promising "the best poem I have yet had or seen from an American" and describing Eliot as "the only American I know of who has made what I can call adequate preparation for writing." The poem which he sent was, of course, "The Love Song of J. Alfred Prufrock." After reading it, Miss Monroe objected to it generally as being too much like Henry James, "correct to the *n*th degree," and in particular disliked the paragraph about Hamlet and the note of futility on which it closed. She showed it to Fletcher, whose verdict was that it seemed "very, very Huefferish and tailed off

[11] "The Renaissance: I—The Palette," *Poetry*, Vol. V, No. 5 (February, 1915), 233.

[12] Quoted by Anderson, *My Thirty Years' War*, 169.

[13] Quoted by Monroe, *A Poet's Life*, 394.

badly towards the conclusion," though he thought it good.[14] Pound was inclined to agree about the Hamlet reference, but he wrote that Eliot wanted it and further scored her for trying to change the Prufrock of the last lines into a "reformed character breathing out fire and ozone." "Prufrock" appeared as Eliot wished, and Pound congratulated *Poetry's* editor:

In being the first magazine to print Eliot you have scored again. He has intelligence and won't get stuck in one hole. You mark my blossoming word—that young chap will go quite a long way. He and Masters are the best of the "bilin."[15]

In addition to continuing his efforts to find poets who were doing competent work, Pound persisted in the search for publication outlets. He was largely responsible for *Blast* No. 2, which appeared in July, 1915, and presented, among others, poems by Eliot. But Vorticism had lost its followers and weakened rather than strengthened Pound's position; it was futile to continue its publication. While the *Some Imagist Poets* series had made the Imagist title useless, it had proved the value of an anthology, and Pound decided once again to try this method of presenting the poetry he felt the public should know about. In 1915 he brought out his second anthology. Called *Catholic Anthology*, it avoided reference to any school. There was no manifesto or preface, nor was the volume preceded by any statement of principles. The contributors shared only Pound's judgment that they were, among modern poets, the most

---

[14] Miss Monroe's reaction to "Prufrock" and his own are described by Fletcher in an unpublished letter to Amy Lowell, December 22, 1914.

[15] Quoted by Monroe, *A Poet's Life*, 368.

significant. After a prefatory sonnet by Yeats, the volume opened with Eliot's "Prufrock." The Imagists were represented only by Williams, Upward, and, indirectly, Hulme (Pound translated into free verse portions of a conversation he had had with Hulme in a war hospital). Perhaps the most surprising was the representation from the United States, where Pound had recently discovered signs of what he considered real ability. He included poems by Edgar Lee Masters and Carl Sandburg, as well as by Orrick Johns, Alfred Kreymborg, Alice Corbin, and Harriet Monroe. He would not have Vachel Lindsay, though: "I don't say he copies Marinetti, but he is with him, and his work is futurist, it is also headed for the popular which is, in the end, hell."

But the anthology was no substitute for a regular magazine outlet. Pound had lost some of his influence in this direction since Aldington had increased his authority with *The Egoist*. When the *Academy* had to seek a backer in 1915, Pound tried to buy it, but could not raise the £500 which the magazine needed. Amy Lowell, however, inadvertently solved his problem: she persisted in advising Harriet Weaver to get rid of Dora Marsden; Miss Weaver finally took offense, and turned to Pound rather than to the Aldingtons for advice. Though Aldington, after he entered the army, carried on his duties as assistant editor through his wife and held the title nominally until June, 1917, H. D. was not able to continue after this date, and Pound took advantage of the situation to have Eliot appointed in Aldington's place.

In America, too, Pound strengthened his magazine connections, which were weakened by his gradual estrangement from *Poetry*. Margaret Anderson's *Little Review* gave him not only an American outlet but one which he approved more than he had *Poetry*. Its first issue announced its aim "to produce criticism of books, music, art, drama, and life that shall be fresh and constructive, and intelligent from the artist's point of view." He had watched the magazine and in 1917 wrote Miss Anderson suggesting that *The Little Review* employ him as foreign editor: "*The Little Review* is perhaps temperamentally closer to what I want done?"[16] She accepted the suggestion and almost immediately the magazine became the American sponsor for the work of Eliot, Lewis, Joyce, and Pound. Part of his new authority with *The Egoist* and later with *The Little Review* he owed to the New York lawyer and patron of the arts, John Quinn. Quinn sent Pound money to pay his contributors, and not only gave money to *The Little Review*, to which he was introduced by Pound, but defended its editor in the *Ulysses* trial.

Pound maintained certain reservations about Miss Lowell. He would not have her around *The Little Review* unless she was willing to contribute heavily from her income and unless her work was confined to sections over which he had no control. Actually, though, he still had little feeling of personal hostility; Damon has pointed out that when he heard from Miss Anderson of Miss Lowell's refusal to publish in *The Little Review* and *The Egoist* because of their connections with him, he wrote her and put their relations back on a more amicable basis. By 1917 they could both be satisfied with their progress: she had guided Imagism into prominence and at the same time had increased her reputation as a poet; he had enabled many young writers to start their careers, bringing recognition to such names as Lewis, Eliot, and Joyce, even while develop-

[16] Quoted by Anderson, *My Thirty Years' War*, 159.

ing his own art. America's entry into the war put an end to the Imagist movement and a temporary halt to the surging interest in the arts that had almost reached the proportions of his desired *risorgimento;* not until the twenties would the renaissance appear in full strength.

III

T. E. Hulme as Imagist

ULME has been called the first Imagist poet and the movement's theorist. The Imagists themselves were the first so to describe him. Pound started it in *Ripostes* and (obliquely) in *Des Imagistes* and the *Catholic Anthology* by associating Imagism with the discussion of the image carried on in Hulme's 1909 club. Flint, in his "History of Imagism," not only confirmed the rather vague assertions of Pound, but went on to deny Imagism any originality other than the originality of Hulme, and most literary histories have accepted his word.

The argument is not completely convincing. Pound was never specific in acknowledging his debt to Hulme; Flint's "History" was not impartial or disinterested—he was annoyed that Pound should take credit for ideas he thought were not his own, and said as much in a letter to Amy Lowell. Both he and Aldington, who requested the "History," intended that it should deflate Pound's expansive pride as the founder of a new school of poetry. And while the parallels between certain theories of the Imagist manifestoes and passages from Hulme's notes are inescapable, they are not clear and conclusive enough to support the indebtedness usually claimed. More detailed study of Hulme's aesthetic and his experimental poems and comparison of these with the Imagism of the anthologies make it by no means certain that Imagism is simply a watered-down version of the *Speculations*, or, if one wishes, a reduction of their principles to essentials.

Before 1913, Hulme seems to have been primarily interested in poetry. He did not remain long with the Poets' Club of 1908, but the group organized in 1909 was certainly exposed to his poetic theory: Flint attended regularly, Pound occasionally. The *salon* which grew out of these meetings attracted a much larger circle, but for that reason probably limited the effectiveness of Hulme's proselyting. Flint, Aldington, and Pound were present frequently, though Pound has stated that it was an unsatisfactory place to discuss poetry. Probably their attendance was due more to a desire for general conversation than to the hope of hearing Hulme elaborate his ideas.

Hulme published no articles exclusively concerned with poetics, and did little lecturing. He spoke before an audience at the Poetry Bookshop in the summer of 1912 on "The New Philosophy of Art as Illustrated in Poetry"; and in 1914 he was one of a series of lecturers in Kensington Town Hall on new developments in art and literature, reading a paper on modern poetry. On this occasion, Wyndham Lewis also appeared in support of Hulme, and Pound illustrated the points of both speakers by reciting some of his and Hulme's poems. Michael Roberts quotes one of the audience:

Hulme was not a good lecturer, and Wyndham Lewis read a paper supporting Hulme and came off pretty badly himself, mumbling in a husky voice, with his head buried in his manuscript. The audience felt as if they could snatch the papers from the poets and read them for themselves—there was so obviously something very worthwhile buried in all their abstract mumbling. To end it all, Ezra Pound stood up, all self-possessed, complete in velvet coat, flowing tie, pointed beard and halo of fiery hair. Lolling against the stage, he became very witty and fluent, and with his Yankee voice snarled out some of his and Hulme's poems. Somehow, such a voice rather clowned verse.[1]

It seems probable that many of his contemporaries knew of Hulme as a theorist, but that few of them knew much about his theory. They must have been acquainted with fragments of it, but he did not have the opportunity to publicize it frequently or systematically enough to root it firmly in their minds. On the other hand, the Imagists Flint, Aldington, and Pound must have known Hulme's theories better than did most of his contemporaries; they were interested in poetry and, especially Flint and Pound, had many opportunities to discuss the subject with him.

The second poets' club developed into the *salon* of 1913–14 as Hulme's interest was turning to modern art, and the salon reflects this trend. The impression of contemporaries is that Hulme was more concerned with the visual arts than with poetry: his friends were principally painters and sculptors, and probably his closest friend was the sculptor Jacob Epstein. The *salon* was preceded by a regular dinner with several of the artists, and topics of interest to them dominated the Frith Street evenings. He defended Epstein against the violent criticism occasioned by his work for the British Medical Association Building and for the

[1] Michael Roberts, *T. E. Hulme* (London, 1938), 21–22.

Wilde Memorial in Paris, and in a brief series of *New Age* articles upheld the modern, geometrical, nonrepresentative art.

> I am attempting in this new series of articles to define the characteristics of a new constructive geometric art which seems to me to be emerging at the present moment.[2]

He further publicized the cause by persuading Orage to reproduce in *The New Age* some of the drawings of Epstein, Gaudier, Nevinson, Roberts, and David Bomberg. However, Michael Roberts has pointed to what was probably the only tangible result of all this enthusiasm: that Epstein's drawing, "The Rock Drill," as well as his carvings in flenite, and some of the early sculpture of Gaudier-Brzeska might be taken to show the influence of Hulme's theories.

Hulme became known, then, less through the poetry clubs and his poetic theory than through the Frith Street *salon* and his theories on the new art; and it was not until 1914 that he found some demand for his lectures. At this time he was forced to drop out of the circles where his theories were gaining respect; England entered the war in the summer, and Hulme joined the service toward the close of the year. Not only were most minds turned to matters other than aesthetics, but Hulme was not able to be in London for periods long enough to consolidate what position he had established for himself, even had he so desired. While he cannot be considered a prominent critic and theorist of the years 1908–17, neither can he be dismissed as a thinker

---

[2] "Modern Art—I," *The New Age*, Vol. XIV, No. 11 (January 15, 1914), 341.

of no significance for the artists of the period; and although his poetic theory had only a limited circulation, it is hardly possible that at least two of the Imagists, Flint and Pound, should have failed to become familiar with it. Imagism *could* have had its source in Hulme.

Hulme analyzed in some detail what he considered the two main problems of the artist. One involves perception, or what he sees; the other involves expression, or how he communicates what he sees. The ordinary man, he said, perceives only with reference to present or future action; that is, he sees not *the* table, but *a* table, classifying objects with reference to immediate or potential use. The artist, however, sees not stock types, but individuals. His problem is to see things as they really are, apart from any conventional way of seeing them. Literature, in fact, may be defined as "entirely the deliberate standing still, hovering and thinking oneself into an artificial view, for the moment, and not effecting any real actions at all."

The literary artist has next to "bend" language to express his unconventional vision. It must be bent to his use because words are designed to serve an essentially practical purpose. They are tags or labels which we give to objects of perception and their function is primarily to classify. By its nature, the process leads to compromise and to conventional expression, because it abstracts from an object the characteristics it has in common with other objects and classifies it on this basis. Consequently, a word tends to give a lowest common denominator of meaning. Its meaning is further conditioned by the fact that it serves not only in perception but in communication, where a similar process takes place. A word is a medium for exchange of information between men, and the extent of the information it conveys is determined by a general agreement that a word means this or that. It circulates at a fixed value, though to individuals it may have other values outside the agreed area. Both the perceptual and communicative uses of words emphasize the abstract rather than the individual; words tend to assume the characteristics of counters that can be moved about upon a chess board.

The artist's second problem, then, is to break the stiff, general patterns which make language incapable of expressing an individual, personal reaction. Instead of conveying only part of an emotion, the part representing the agreed area of meaning, he seeks to convey the full range of his own individual feeling; he endeavors to express what lies outside the circle represented by the word as a counter. His success depends directly upon his ability to use metaphor, because by revealing new analogies to the reader he can convey the freshness and individuality of new vision.

The function of analogy in poetry may be summed up as follows: "to enable one to dwell and linger upon a point of excitement":

The inner psychology of a poet at such a creative moment is like that of a drunkard who pushes his hand forward along a table, with an important gesture, and remains there pondering over it. In that relaxing gesture of pushing comes the inner psychology of all these moments.[3]

Two characteristics of analogy not only permit but force the reader to linger over points significant to the poet. One is the concrete, visual quality of the imagery used in the comparison. "Each word must be an image *seen*, not a

[3] "Notes on Language and Style," 292; I have used the notes published by Michael Roberts as Appendix III in *T. E. Hulme*.

counter."[4] The image is a representation of a physical object, and the reader reacts to it in the same way he would to a physical object. A direct, personal reaction eliminates the need for poet and reader to communicate through the leveling medium of ordinary counter words. Further, the physical thing evokes in the reader an emotion he feels as his own, and he is therefore inclined to linger over it with more pleasure. A poetry of images "endeavors to arrest you, and to make you continuously see a physical thing, to prevent you gliding through an abstract process."[5]

Concreteness of imagery insures freshness, but so does the novelty of an original juxtaposition of images, the second source of the analogy's strength. It produces a shock of recognition that also brings the reader to an abrupt stop. The effect Hulme wanted was one that would set poetry apart from the practical and dully reasonable attitudes of normal life. "Never, never, never a simple statement. It has no effect. Always must have analogies, which make an other-world through the glass effect, which is what I want."[6] The theory sets art squarely to the task of creating, not imitating; "beauty does not exist by itself in nature, waiting to be copied, only organized pieces of cinders."[7]

Hulme hoped to give his faith in analogy a sound basis by arguing that thought is "the simultaneous presentation to the mind of two different images ... merely the discovery of new analogies, when useful and sincere, and not mere paradoxes."[8] His argument oversimplifies for the sake of staying on "easily defined routes"; doubtless he would not

[4] *Ibid.*, 274.
[5] *Speculations* (New York, 1924), 134.
[6] "Notes on Language and Style," 285–86.
[7] *Ibid.*, 299.
[8] *Ibid.*, 281.

have insisted upon the unqualified statement that one thinks solely in terms of images. But he certainly would have given up only a part of his proposition. He was convinced that the imaging process must be present in good writing. "A man cannot write without seeing at the same time a visual signification before his eyes. It is this image which precedes the writing and makes it firm."[9]

Hulme has asserted a debt to Henri Bergson for certain points in his aesthetic; and as one studies the aesthetic, he finds an approach and a subsequent, hasty retreat from Bergson which is characteristic of Hulme's philosophy as a whole. Hulme began by adopting certain conclusions as a point of departure for an analysis of what one feels in art; he cited two aspects of Bergsonism which he considered important for aesthetics. One is the conception of reality as a flux of interpenetrated elements unseizable by the intellect; the other is the orientation of the mind toward action and the significance of this orientation for the normal habits of operation which the human mind has developed. The mind or intellect apprehends external phenomena in such a way that man can act on them, not so that he can know them; it places a veil between man and reality. It is the artist who, emancipated from the necessity for action, can lift the veil and expose reality. He does not ask, "How can I put this to my own use?" but, "How does this reveal the inner life of things?" While normal perception sees the features of a living being as "assembled, not as mutually organized," and misses the intention of life that runs through them and gives them significance, this "intention is just what the artist tries to regain ... in breaking down ... the barrier that space puts up between him and his model."[10] This is the

[9] *Ibid.*

basis for Hulme's statement of the artist's problem of perception.

Bergson also provided Hulme with an analysis of language which revealed the limitations imposed upon it by its service to the intellect and its consequent inability to express what the artist sees. He admitted that language has contributed generously to intelligence. Without it, intellect would have remained fixed on the external objects with which it deals, and would never have been freed for more complex processes of thought. Yet its service has seriously restricted its power to express what is beyond the confines of intellect. It cannot, for example, adequately express a reality like consciousness, because consciousness is made up of interpenetrated states. Language, conditioned by the analytical habits of intellect, spreads out in space what depends for its identity upon an interpenetration. It can express reality only in non-real terms.

Finally Bergson had also solved the problem of communication in terms of the image or analogy. Faced with the difficulty of expressing the "unique" and "inexpressible," his philosophy relied heavily upon striking analogies. He did not believe that images can express reality fully or even partially, but he was convinced that they provide the only means by which man can approach the point where he will be forced to surrender to it.

No image can replace the intuition of duration, but many diverse images, borrowed from very different orders of things, may, by the convergence of their action, direct consciousness to the precise point where there is a certain intuition to be seized.[11]

[10] *Creative Evolution* (New York, 1911), 177.
[11] *An Introduction to Metaphysics* (New York, 1912), 16.

The artist prepares the way for intuition by lulling the active and resistant powers of intellect and creating a state of mind receptive to suggestion. For example, a poet employs both imagery and rhythm to gain his effect.

The poet is he with whom feelings develop into images, and the images themselves into words which translate them while obeying the laws of rhythm.[12]

Through the rhythms of his words, he can subdue the intellect and prepare the way for an intuition. He not only has the command of the image, he can create conditions which increase its effectiveness.

One is still on ground of agreement between Hulme and Bergson. A passage from Hulme's "Lecture on Modern Poetry" is clearly an echo of Bergson on the poet's method:

Say the poet is moved by a certain landscape, he selects from that certain images which, put into juxtaposition in separate lines, serve to suggest and evoke the state he feels. To this piling-up and juxtaposition of distinct images in different lines, one can find a fanciful analogy in music. A great revolution in music when, for the melody that is one-dimensional music, was substituted harmony which moves in two. Two visual images form what one may call a visual chord. They unite to suggest an image which is different to both.[13]

The parallels bear out Hulme's statement that he was indebted to Bergson for providing his roughly formulated aesthetic with an efficient vocabulary. Both theorists insisted

[12] *Time and Free Will* (New York, 1910), 15.
[13] Roberts, *T. E. Hulme*, 266 (Appendix II).

that the poet's vision is an unconventional one, adjudged language incompetent to express it, and relied upon metaphor and analogy to bring the reader into range of the vision's effectiveness. But Hulme's debt is limited to Bergson's lucid argument of these related ideas; beyond this the theories of the two men are at wide variance.

According to Bergson, the artist sees reality. He escapes the mind's normal orientation toward action and turns instead to the search for pure knowledge; he has learned that intuition serves where intellect fails. Through intuition, he discerns in the face of a living being, for example, the

intention of life, the simple movement that runs through the lines, that binds them together and gives them significance. This intention is just what the artist tries to regain, in placing himself back within the object by a kind of sympathy, in breaking down, by an effort of intuition, the barrier that space puts up between him and his model.

Bergson was so certain of the existence of intuition in aesthetics that he relied upon it to explain what he meant by his metaphysical use of the term, pointing to the phenomenon which frequently occurs when one has gathered all of his materials and is prepared for writing. Before one can begin effectively, there must be an intuition which suddenly forces the work forward in a specific direction, the words falling into place as he proceeds. Bergson even cited the aesthetic in *proof* of the possibility that the metaphysical exists: "That an effort of this kind is not impossible, is proved by the existence in man of an aesthetic faculty along with normal perception."[14]

[14] *Creative Evolution*, 176–77.

57

Hulme's philosophy is marked by a consistent refusal to grant to intuition the powers Bergson gave it, and he defined literature as the "hovering and thinking oneself into an *artificial view*," hardly a phrase one would apply to reality.[15] Recall for a moment his defense of analogy: it evokes a physical and thus an individual reaction, and it startles the reader out of his normal habits of thought by presenting relations unseen before. It avoids the abstract and makes language a sharp instrument with which to probe human feelings. Although he wrote, "Images in verse are not mere decoration, but the very essence of an intuitive language,"[16] there is no evidence that the artist knows or puts his audience in touch with any reality except that which can be defined in the relative terms of a sense of existence newly freshened and recharged with immediacy by the sudden apprehension of unexpected likeness.

Hulme described literature as either *romantic* or *classic*. The terms carry into his aesthetic the same meaning they had in his philosophy, and represent opposing views of what the artist sees, what constitutes his vision. The romantic assumes that the human mind can apprehend the realities of religion as well as those of the external world; he is the humanist, who, assuming a continuity between the world of absolute truths and the world of intellect, tends to explain the religious in human terms and reduce God to the level of man. He believes in man as a measure of all things and consequently in the doctrines of individualism, progress, and perfectibility. The classicist refuses to view man so optimistically; he assumes a discontinuity between the areas of religious, absolute truth and of mind or intellect.

[15] "Notes on Languages and Style," 296.
[16] *Speculations*, 135.

He argues that the "gaps" can be bridged not by the intellect, but by intuition, and is unwilling to grant intuition any but occasional efficacy. He believes God the absolute measure of all things, man subordinate and rigidly limited in his power to apprehend reality.

As romantics, he pointed to Keats, Coleridge, Byron, Shelley, and Swinburne. Characteristically, he neglected to analyze the work of each poet to support his classification, proceeding instead to speak in general terms, and leaving the reader to perform the detailed criticism for himself. Of the romantics, he wrote:

Verse to them always means a bringing in of some of the emotions that are grouped round the word infinite . . . I object to the sloppiness which doesn't consider that a poem is a poem unless it is moaning or whining about something or other.[17]

Believing that man reflects and can comprehend the divine, the romantic poet likes to treat ideas and emotions that he thinks representative of divinity or at least of the mysterious forces of the universe. He likes to talk of the soul and of the realities above those of practical, everyday life, suggesting easy comprehension where there is none.

If I use the word soul, or speak of higher realities, . . . you will know that at that precise point I didn't know of any real reason and was trying to bluff you.[18]

Attempting to convey an idea of the infinite, which man is theoretically capable of understanding, the romantic crashes

[17] *Ibid.*, 126–27.
[18] "Lecture on Modern Poetry," in Roberts, *T. E. Hulme*, 258–59.

headlong into the fact that not language but comprehension fails him, and he takes refuge in a technique which depends upon the impressiveness of mystery and evasion. Instead of admitting the absolute, inscrutable mystery of reality, he makes a fetish of the mystery and believes that he is thus dealing with reality itself.

Escapes to the infinite:
(i)   Art. Blur, Strangeness, music.
(ii) Sentimentality.[19]

Sentimentality is another characteristic of romantic verse. Individualism encourages an abnormal care for one's own feelings; personal emotions are given an importance, a significance and sanctity, which they do not deserve. Further, the tendency of the romantic is toward the more lugubrious emotions: he "moans" about the way man is oppressed by society, he "whines" about his inability to use himself to the full extent consistent with his divine nature. "The thing has got so bad now that a poem which is all dry and hard . . . would not be considered poetry at all. Poetry that isn't damp isn't poetry at all."[20] The romantic attitude, in short, makes literature a falsehood.

The literary man deliberately perpetrates a hypocrisy, in that he fits together his own isolated moments of ecstasy (and generally deliberate use of big words without personal meaning attached) and presents them as pictures of higher life, thereby giving old maids a sense of superiority to other people and giving mandarins the opportunity to talk of "ideals." Then makes at-

[19] *Speculations,* 232.
[20] *Ibid.,* 126–27.

tempt to justify himself by inventing the soul and saying that occasionally the lower world gets glimpses of this, and that inferentially he is the medium. As a matter of fact, being certain moments of ecstasy perhaps brought on by drink.[21]

The classicists include Horace, most of the Elizabethans, and the Augustans. Hulme described classical verse in terms of the philosophical attitude from which he drew the name:

even in the most imaginative flights there is always a holding back, a reservation. The classical poet never forgets this finiteness, this limit of man. He remembers always that he is mixed up with earth. He may jump, but he always returns back; he never flies away into the circumambient gas.[22]

In order to encompass poets of such diverse techniques as the Elizabethans and the Augustans, Hulme found it necessary to distinguish between static and dynamic classicism. The dynamic includes the Elizabethans and, in particular, Shakespeare—even his most imaginative and logically preposterous metaphors are presented with a flourish and an amused detachment.

The distinction between romantic and classical verse was not an academic point with Hulme. It was his way of distinguishing in poetic theory between the foolish over-estimation of man's potentialities which extends his vision to include reality, and the wise foreshortening of his vision which also accepts the foreshortening with good grace. It represented a plea and a prophecy. The terms in which he described the two types of verse eloquently argued his be-

[21] "Notes on Language and Style," 303.
[22] *Speculations*, 120.

lief that the poet should reject the romantic and turn to the classic, and he confidently predicted that a reform was about to take place.

I want to maintain that after a hundred years of romanticism, we are in for a classical revival. . . . I prophesy that a period of dry, hard, classical verse is coming.[23]

He made specific suggestions for the guidance of poets who wished to achieve the "cheerful, dry and sophisticated" tone of the new verse, and even wrote a handful of poems to demonstrate his theories.

Perhaps Hulme's most sweeping recommendation restricted the subject matter of poetry. As man is a limited creature who cannot know reality, it is vain to insist that his art reveal the truths of the universe. Since "we no longer believe in perfection, either in verse or in thought, we frankly acknowledge the relative."[24] Instead of trying to communicate perfection, the classicist attempts to communicate an individual, personal mood. Hulme excluded as inappropriate and romantic the vast, vague emotions loosely grouped under the adjective *inspirational:* poetry, he said, is not religion, nor have the two any aims in common; it is not designed to impel men toward Progress. The aim is to express the vivid patches, the "sudden lifts" in life, "cf. love, fighting, dancing. The moments of ecstasy."[25]

Speaking of personal matters, the first time I ever felt the necessity or inevitableness of verse, was in the desire to reproduce the

[23] *Ibid.,* 113, 137.
[24] "Lecture on Modern Poetry," 264.
[25] "Notes on Language and Style," 302.

peculiar quality of feeling which is induced by the flat spaces and wide horizons of the virgin prairie of western Canada.[26]

It would be a mistake to interpret the "sudden lift" or the emotion evoked by the Canadian landscape as in any way associated with the ecstasy of the romantic poets. The feelings that Hulme wanted poetry to express were the minor, transient, almost trivial ones which result from seeing physical things in an unconventional way. And although poetry is most intense when dealing with the vivid patches inspired by love and fighting, it does not have to wait for their appearance. Any new way of seeing objects of routine existence is worth expression.

The effort of the literary man to find subtle analogies for the ordinary street feelings he experiences leads to the differentiation and importance of those feelings. What would be unnoticed by others, and is nothing when not labelled, becomes an important emotion. A transitory artificial impression is deliberately cultivated into an emotion and written about. Reason here creates and modifies an emotion, *e.g.* standing at street corners. Hence the sudden joy these produce in the reader when he remembers a half-forgotten impression, "How true!"[27]

Hulme tends to reduce poetry almost to the creation of sophisticated *bons mots*. Convinced of man's ineffectiveness as a seer who can reveal the mystery of the universe, Hulme insisted that he turn his eyes from searching the horizon to examining a limited area around his feet. There is nothing "new under the sun," and all literature is an

26 "Lecture on Modern Poetry," 266.
27 "Notes on Language and Style," 295.

accident, a happy escape from platitude. . . . Literature like pitching, how to throw phrases about, to satisfy a demand. An exercise for the time being, no eternal body to be added to.[28]

After all, poetry is "for the amusement of bankers and other sedentary armchair people in after-dinner moods. No other." The following comprises its range of usefulness:

(i) amuse banker
(ii) for use of clerks in love to send to sweethearts
(iii) temporary moods (in theatres) of cultivated people
(iv) songs of war.[29]

If the classical poet's art consists of making the phenomena of everyday life poetic by presenting them in an unusual way, he will have to rely on analogy. A single original comparison sharpens interest where the most colorful and concentrated description fails. The distinctive characteristic of Hulme's conception of analogy is his obsession with the solid physical sensations it can convey. *"It is the physical analogies that hold me, . . .* not the *vain* decorative and verbal images of the ordinary poets. . . . The process of invention is that of gradually making solid the castles in the air."[30]

In "Cinders" he had made some effort to give his preoccupation with the physical a philosophical basis. He expressed a belief that the soul is "undifferentiated," that it is given personality through the body. One's being, so far as he knows, is simply the accumulation of feelings produced by reactions of the body to various stimuli. Emotion

[28] *Ibid.*, 283.
[29] *Ibid.*, 293.
[30] *Ibid.*, 276.

is physical in nature and depends "on real solid vision or sound." Consequently the poet will express himself in terms of physical sensations, the kind of knowledge that affects men most deeply and directly. "All poetry is an affair of the body—that is, to be real it must affect the body."[31] Of course, the sensations conveyed by poetry cannot equal in intensity those experienced directly, because feeling is filtered through language; but poetry can be an effective "compromise for a language of intuition which would hand over sensations bodily."

With perfect style, the solid leather for reading, each sentence should be a lump, a piece of clay, a vision seen; rather, a wall touched with soft fingers. Never should one feel light vaporous bridges between one solid sense and another. No bridges—all solid; then never exasperated. . . . Always seek the hard, definite, personal word.[32]

The primary weapon of the classical poet in the invention of new analogies is fancy. Dealing with "finite things," it can produce the kind of imagery which Hulme felt essential to effective verse. He insisted upon a clearly defined distinction between fancy and imagination, with which it is sometimes confused: "where you get the [creative or artistic impulse] exhibited in the realm of emotions you get imagination, and . . . where you get this quality exhibited in the contemplation of finite things you get fancy."[33] Originally, he said, the words *fancy* and *imagination* had been synonymous, but they had been differentiated by eighteenth-

[31] *Speculations*, 242.
[32] "Notes on Language and Style," 275; *Speculations*, 231.
[33] *Speculations*, 134.

century German writers on aesthetics. Thereafter imagination had become the shibboleth of the poets he described as romantic and had become associated with the characteristics of their work. Its connotations of emotionalism as well as of social and artistic lawlessness made it a word extremely unpleasant to Hulme's ear; fancy, on the other hand, seemed to suggest the control and precision which Hulme wanted in poetry. The distinction was a convenient way to justify his own poetic tastes.

Convenient though it may have been, it was not very effective because Hulme did not offer a detailed exposition of what he meant by the words. His references to them leave some question whether he really meant to draw so clear a line between them and dismiss imagination as a faculty detrimental to poetry. On one occasion he contrasted intellect, which can deal with complexities of the mechanical kind, can produce intricate diagrams and patterns, with fancy, which can create from its material an organic product whose nature cannot be explained simply by analysis of its parts. The contrast, of course, applies to aesthetics the manifolds theory Hulme had found so useful in philosophy. As in metaphysics it had allowed for the appearance of phenomena unpredictable in the mechanistic terms of cause and effect, so in aesthetics it allowed for the existence of a truly creative element above the mere organization of materials. Hulme believed that art is creative, that its value derives from more than mechanical arrangement of form; he had therefore to attribute some such ability to fancy since he had categorically condemned imagination. As Michael Roberts has pointed out, the result is that Hulme's fancy is similar to the romantic definition of imagination made by Coleridge. Fancy appears to be imagination with its egotism deflated, its emotion held in check by reason, and, one suspects, its attitude tempered by a sense of humor.

Hulme established a reasonable standard for evaluating the new verse. If its function is to communicate a personal feeling or physical sensation, its measure as good or bad verse must reside in the effectiveness with which it conveys this feeling. One can define art as "a passionate desire for accuracy, and the essentially aesthetic emotion as the excitement which is generated by direct communication."[34] Verse is not an occult art, exempt from the demands of clarity. It is "simply and solely the means of expression . . . just as prose is, and if you can't justify it from that point of view it's not worth preserving."[35] In fact, its difference from prose is only a matter of degree. It is more efficient than prose because it is the advance guard which creates the images that give language its freshness and directness. Poetry

chooses fresh epithets and fresh metaphors, not so much because they are new and we are tired of the old, but because the old cease to convey a physical thing and become abstract counters.[36]

Prose, in Hulme's vocabulary, was simply a word to describe language whose imagery has gone stale. "Prose is . . . the museum where the dead images of verse are preserved."[37] Bad poetry is prose no matter how perfect it may be metrically.

But he did not think the question of metrics irrelevant. He recommended that the classical poet seek a new verse

[34] *Ibid.*, 162.
[35] "Lecture on Modern Poetry," 258.
[36] "Searchers After Reality," *The New Age*, Vol. V, No. 17 (August 19, 1909), 315.
[37] *Ibid.*

form and pointed to specific defects in the old which encouraged a verse that appealed to the ear and frequently had no effect other than to lull the faculties of the mind into a mild condition of hypnosis. Even more serious, it restricted the poet's choice of the most accurate language in which to clothe his metaphor. The new verse, depending as it does upon images which strike the eye and arrest the mind, demands a free and elastic metrical pattern. "I contend that this method of recording impressions by visual images in distinct lines does not require the old metric system."[38] The implication is that what the new method does require is a form similar to the French *vers libre*, and the two of its principles which Hulme chose to mention were those that would best suit Imagism: denial of a regular number of syllables as the basis for versification; determination of line length by the requirements of the imagery, the contours of the poet's thought.

Although his emphasis upon imagery suggested an argument against traditional metrical patterns, this was not the ostensible reason offered for rejecting them. "The principle on which I rely in this paper is that there is an intimate connection between the verse form and the state of poetry at any period."[39] It is usually true but seldom recognized that an efflorescence of verse in a given period can be traced to the invention or introduction of a new verse form. Hulme attributed the lively interest in poetry among the Elizabethans to their discovery of blank verse and the contemporary renaissance in French poetry to Kahn's statement of the principles of *vers libre*. He believed in the value of a new form per se.

[38] *"Lecture on Modern Poetry,"* 267.
[39] *Ibid.,* 259–60.

One might sum it all up in this way: a shell is a very suitable covering for the egg at a certain period of its career, but very unsuitable at a later age. . . . I will conclude, ladies and gentlemen, by saying, the shell must be broken.[40]

Hulme's poems are not merely unimaginative exercises written to the specifications of a blueprint. While they are clearly meant to demonstrate his theory, they do not need the theory to justify their appearance in print; and while they conform to his recommendations, they place them in a perspective that suggests their relative importance, and in at least one case they reveal clearly a significant point which would probably be overlooked on the strength of his theory alone.

The poems deal with the subjects of everyday perception:

Above the quiet dock in midnight,
Tangled in the tall mast's corded height,
Hangs the moon. What seemed so far away
Is but a child's balloon, forgotten after play.[41]

or:

Alluring, earth-seducing, with high conceits
is the sunset that coquettes
at the end of westward streets.

A sudden flaring sky
troubling strangely the passer-by
with vision, alien to long streets, of Cytherea,
or the smooth flesh of Lady Castlemaine. . . .

[40] *Ibid.,* 270.
[41] "Above the Dock," *Speculations,* 266.

69

A frolic of crimson
is the spreading glory of the sky
heaven's wanton
flaunting a trailed red robe
along the fretted city roofs
about the time of homeward-going crowds
—a vain maid, lingering, loth to go....[42]

The subjects are not only conventional perceptually, but are "standard" material for poetry. Perhaps Hulme selected them for both characteristics, because his intent was to force the reader to see an object apart from a normal, or practical, and a stylized, or literary, way of seeing it. In any case, the poems show him following literally his own advice on the choice of subject matter. He deals not with vast emotions or with the problems of the universe, but with the very personal feelings that result from viewing a physical object in an unusual way.

The originality and freshness of feeling are conveyed by analogy. The poems make no pretense of demanding more attention than the analogies on which they are based seem to warrant. Success or failure depends wholly upon effectiveness of imagery. The imagery is, however, slightly different from what one would have expected. While Hulme emphasizes the importance of the purely physical aspects of the image and its effect upon the reader's feelings, and while his theory thus seems to argue for a richly sensuous verse, he uses the physical object in such a way that its "hardness" is only one consideration. His plea for a poetry that would appeal to the senses was not intended to encourage what is ordinarily understood as sensuous poetry, and

[42] "A City Sunset," *T. E. Hulme*, 257.

the poems show that the object is important not only because it is physical, but because its peculiar nature completes a contrast. One finds the moon compared to a child's balloon, a sunset compared to a coquettish girl, the stars to the white faces of town children, and the sky described in these lines:

> *Oh, God, make small*
> *The old star-eaten blanket of the sky,*
> *That I may fold it round me and in comfort lie.*[43]

The comparison in each case reduces a normally "poetic" and impressive perception to the level of the trivia of everyday life. The reduction, of course, works to the advantage of both: the poetic loses its conventional stiffness and artificiality and the trivial becomes suddenly worthy of notice.

The total effect conveys a freshness, which was what Hulme admittedly sought, mingled with a feeling of amusement and usually irony, of which he made little in his theory. He did say on one occasion: "Analogies in poetry, like the likenesses of babies, to be taken half seriously, with a smile,"[44] but this is the only reference to an aspect of analogy that shows up in his poems and is fundamental to his aesthetic as far as it pertains to poetry. His philosophy, wavering between admission and denial of man's ability to know reality, never wholly entered the area of admission; the section of *Speculations* entitled "Cinders" almost flatly refused to grant him the power. His poems accept the tragic nature of man's limitations with an ironic amusement that shows most clearly in the kind of contrast he expected analogy to make. The physical object not only in-

[43] "The Embankment," *Speculations*, 267.
[44] "Notes on Language and Style," 283.

sures a concise reaction, but, being trivial, reduces the lofty to insignificance and produces an effect of amused irony appropriate to the classical attitude and the pessimistic view of "Cinders."

Finally, the poems suggest that Hulme's argument for a new verse form reflects more accurately the requirements of imagism than it does his belief in the value of a new form per se. The poems have no regular metrical pattern. The rhythm is iambic where one can define a pattern, but the metre is ignored where an analogy seems to require it. Line lengths are adjustable to the linguistic demands of the image. Michael Roberts has said that Hulme was not unaware of the importance of sound values in poetry and that in one of his manuscript poems he had carefully marked the accents. Nevertheless, his poems are free of the traditional patterns: imagism seems to be inextricably related, at least in Hulme's practice, to a free verse.

Beyond its immediate interest as a forerunner of Imagism, Hulme's theory of poetry has a more general significance. His defense of an imagist verse (and the statements of the Imagists who followed him), represent a surrender of certain claims—at once a withdrawal from fields of knowledge and communication in which the poet had competed with the scientist and the philosopher and an effort, within narrow and more clearly defined limits, to make the poetic medium more exact and scientific. Hulme and the Imagist mark the beginning of this effort, which culminates in the more complex and elaborate theories of certain contemporary critics, to delineate for poetry an area, distinct and inviolate, in which it can operate without fear of encroachment from other forms of knowledge—to establish a place for poetry in a scientific, machine world. And while Imagism was only a first stage, its assumptions (whether metaphysical—as with Hulme—or aesthetic—as with Pound) have not been wholly replaced; poetry still has some difficulty, for example, in countering satisfactorily its reasons for insisting that the brief lyric is the form most suitable to the contemporary artist.

IV

Imagism and Symbolism

FROM 1912 TO 1918, the Imagists championed the cause of French poetry as ardently as their own. F. S. Flint was the first enthusiast; from 1908 he used his *New Age* review column to publicize the verse of his French contemporaries, contrasting the lively atmosphere in French letters and the high quality of French poetry with the lethargic and tradition-bound attitudes of the English poets and the inferior quality of their work. In 1912, the year he introduced Pound, Aldington, and H. D. to Symbolist verse, he extended his efforts by publishing in *The Poetry Review* a lengthy survey of Symbolist aims and accomplishments, concentrating mainly upon the technique of the younger, living generation. The next year he was invited by Monro to furnish *Poetry and Drama* with a "French Chronicle," which became a feature of each issue; and Harriet Monroe asked for a series of articles of the same kind.

Once Pound recognized the significance of the work being done in France, he, too, became its eloquent advocate. Apparently not much impressed by Flint's proselyting, he found Fletcher more convincing, especially when Fletcher lent him his collection of French poetry, and in 1913 he began to shout his discovery from the columns of *The New Age*. The articles, entitled "Approach to Paris," stated an unqualified approval: "There are just two things in the world, two great and interesting phenomena: the intellectual life of Paris and the curious teething promise of my own vast occidental nation."[1] These early articles also reflected a taste decidedly different from Flint's; Pound, for example, favored De Gourmont, Jammes, and Corbière, and passed casually over Verhaeren, whose *Love Poems* Flint translated and whom Flint considered "the greatest European poet of our time."

Pound also carried on his propagandizing through *Poetry*, though he found Miss Monroe unreceptive to an argument for a French section edited by a French correspondent. He summarized for her the judgments offered in his "Approach to Paris," and contributed articles on De Gourmont, Verhaeren, Laforgue, and others. His most ambitious effort, however, went to *The Little Review*; it was a survey, more extensive even than Flint's *Poetry Review* essay, of all aspects of French poetry with which he felt the average reader should be familiar.

Other Imagists were as much excited, if less vocal. As editor of *The Egoist*, Aldington devoted space to French literature in each number, printing poems in the original and translations of prose. Like Pound and Flint, he contributed to *Poetry* articles designed to keep American readers in touch with literary activity in Paris and also took his case to *The Little Review*, with a 1915 series whose attitude is suggested by his statement that "French poetry is the foremost in our age for fertility, originality, and general poetic charm." Amy Lowell carried French poetry to larger

[1] *The New Age*, Vol. XIII, No. 19 (September 4, 1913), 552.

75

audiences both by her readings and by her *Six French Poets,* which was little concerned with technical criticism and concentrated instead upon the broader appeal of biographical facts and translation. In all, the Imagists showed more than enough interest in Symbolist verse to suggest that their doctrine might have been in some measure shaped by it. That their poems echo or frankly appropriate specific rhythms and imagery from the Symbolists has been clearly demonstrated by M. René Taupin in *L'Influence du symbolisme français;* but too hasty and sweeping an assumption of similarity is misleading.

Symbolism was, even less perhaps than Imagism, a movement of poets united behind a single doctrine; it may include both De Gourmont's *"tout n'est que matière, ou rien n'est matière"* and Rimbaud's belief in the Unknown, which he hoped to comprehend by a *"dérèglement de tous les sens";* both Mallarmé's love of abstraction and Laforgue's precise, if eccentric, imagery. Realizing the danger of generalization here, as with Imagism, one can still define certain fundamentals upon which the Symbolists would have agreed. Moreas' statement, published in 1886 by *Figaro littéraire,* stands as the closest approximation to a Symbolist manifesto:

Ennemie de l'enseignement, la déclamation, la fausse sensibilité, la description objective, la poésie symboliste cherche à vêtir l'Idée d'une forme sensible qui, néanmoins, ne serait pas son but à elle-mêne, mais qui, tout en servant à exprimer l'Idée, demeurait sujette. L'Idée, à son tour, ne doit point se laisser voir privée de ses somptueuses simarres des analogies extérieures; car le caractère essentiel de l'art symbolique consiste à ne jamais aller jusqu'à la concentration de l'Idée en soi. Ainsi, dans cet art, les

*tableaux de la nature, les actions des humains, tous les phé-
nomènes concrets ne sauraient se manifester eux-mêmes; ce sont
là des apparences sensibles destinées à représenter leurs affinités
ésotériques avec des Idées primordiales.*[2]

The importance of the symbol is obvious, for it is a means
of "clothing the Idea in sensible form." Its conventional
use for this end may be seen in the verse of Verlaine, who
wished to capture the elusive qualities of existence glimpsed
in moods of languor and melancholy. A partial list of symbols employed in his poems would include deep-tolling
bells, white fountains sobbing in the moonlight, songs in a
minor key. In *"Chanson d'Automne,"* for example, a bell,
which sounds the hour, brings sad memories of former days,
the poet drifts with the wind like a dead leaf, the whole
scene gently vibrates with the sobs of nature's violins. Nature, as Idea, speaks through the external, evoking the
mood which brings the poet closest to the Idea and providing
the symbols by which the mood may be communicated.

But the symbol, as conventionally understood, was not
an entirely adequate weapon. Conforming to the patterns of
external nature, it kept verse fixed upon the actual and allowed only a limited comprehension of the forces in which
the Symbolists were primarily interested. Not content with
the *approach*, they wished, if they could not convey the Idea
or the mystery itself, to convey certain of its qualities. Since
unreality, inaccessibility, and even obscurity were qualities
of the Real, they were taken over as qualities of Symbolist
verse. A Symbolist poem, then, was intended to suggest
what it could not directly express. Symbol, but also image,
syntax, and prosody were turned to the task.

[2] Quoted by André Barre, *Symbolisme* (Paris, 1911), 110.

Verlaine's emphasis upon the musical possibilities of verse is a case in point. Since the qualities he wished to suggest were to be felt most strongly in elusive and shadowy moods induced by a certain kind of music, he developed a metric which would reproduce its characteristics. Composing lines of an uneven number of syllables, avoiding obvious and traditional rhyme and metre, he produced an apparently disordered but carefully controlled rhythm. He further recommended that the poet sacrifice sense to sound in order that the elements of pitch and duration, as well as rhythm, might aid in creating the effect; and the sense itself was to be shadowy and vague, that the total impression might be the dreamy unreality he desired—as he says in *"Art poétique,"* avoid the fixed, definite color, seek the elusive shade, the nuance.

Mallarmé developed a more complex technique. His Reality may perhaps be described as Idea, but it was the Idea of annihilation, nothingness. Since this reality is partially approximated in the human mind by abstraction, Mallarmé sought to reproduce the qualities of abstraction in his verse. He of course relied heavily upon the abstract word, because he could thus divorce perception from its focus upon the concrete and external; but he sought more positive means of establishing the characteristics of the Idea. *"Le vierge, le vivace, et le bel aujourd'hui"* is built upon a single symbol, a swan imprisoned in the ice, but Mallarmé surrounds the symbol with words which are not only abstract but strongly suggestive of the immobility and lifelessness, the frozen qualities of abstraction itself: *vierge, givre, pur éclat, songe froid de mépris, transparent glacier, stérile hiver, blanche agonie.* *"Petit Air"* uses other devices to create the anti-vital nature of the Idea, apparently on the theory that by transforming the conventionally real into unreality, one at least approximates the Unreal. The scene with which the poem is concerned is established by the negative means of asserting what is *not* present in it *(le cygne* and *le quai)*; the syntax is extremely difficult, being broken and telescoped in one passage (lines 9–14) to reflect almost simultaneous perception of two events; ellipsis (line 12) further hobbles normal communication, although it emphasizes the act of withholding rather than the fact of omission; and the imagery is purposely inexact, either because only a few, incomplete brush strokes are given, or because of the irregular syntax already mentioned. In no sense is the imagery meant to clarify or illuminate, though this does not mean that it leaves no sensuous impression; and, except as the poem as a whole becomes symbol or metaphor expressing the "unreality" of the world of the dream or reverie, there is no symbolism as found in Verlaine or in some of Mallarmé's earlier verse.

Rimbaud's technique was also directed towards suggesting the characteristics of the Mystery, if not the Mystery itself; and he, too, worked upon the principle that one approached absolute unreality by distorting the real. His imagery is precise, detailed, and meticulous in its detail, but it is the imagery of hallucination. By separating the imagination from the controls of logic, language from its conventional referents, he hoped to reveal the Unknown. He became *"maître en fantasmagories"*; he lived in a world of hallucination and *"voyais très franchement une mosquée à la place d'une usine, une école de tambours faite par des anges, des calèches sur les routes du ciel, un salon au fond d'un lac."*[3] In *"Bateau ivre,"* the boat's voyage symbolizes the poet's

[3] *"Une Saison en Enfer,"* Oeuvres (Paris, 1947), 207, 219.

voyage in search of the Unknown (and his subsequent failure), but the poem's fundamental appeal is that of the fantastic realm created by its imagery: giant serpents dangling from twisted trees; sea monsters trapped and rotting; hurricanes and whirlpools; gold, brown, or mother-of-pearl waves—the strange, exotic, and colorful encountered by the boat as it exults in its unfamiliar freedom.

While the Symbolists were poets above all, their aesthetic obviously had a strongly metaphysical tinge. According to Mallarmé, the new poets all met on the common ground of an idealism which rejected both natural materials and any direct statement that might give them order, retaining for poetry nothing but the suggestion which the materials evoked. They were thus participants in the same upsurge of idealism for which Bergson became the spokesman in philosophy. Although Bergson was only a parallel and not a source, his philosophy was a closely reasoned argument for the existence of what the Symbolists thought of as the unknowable and for its absolute difference from ordinary reality; and his statements about art clearly resemble theirs.

One recalls his assertion that the artist's function is to place himself within his subject by an act of intuition and to reveal the unique and inexpressible, the intention of life within it. Because language is functionally incapable of expressing an intuition, the poet cannot directly communicate it, but relies upon the suggestive power of his images and the lulling effect of his rhythm to recreate in the reader the characteristics of the reality, the exact emotional environment in which he was able to apprehend it. The knowledge apprehended by intuition is not precise in the scientific sense, and intuition itself is, in relation to intelligence, what

Bergson describes as "a vague nebulosity." Art "aims at impressing feelings on us rather than expressing them; it suggests them to us, and willingly dispenses with the imitation of nature when it finds some more efficacious means";[4] the beautiful is not a specific quality, and "every feeling suggested and not caused is aesthetic or answers the aesthetic character."[5] Though not as fully developed from a technical standpoint, the theory is substantially the same as that underlying Symbolism; against it one might, for example, set Mallarmé's words: "Nommer *un objet, c'est supprimer les trois-quarts de la jouissance du poème qui est faite du bonheur de deviner peu à peu; le* suggérer *voilà le rêve. C'est le parfait usage de ce mystère qui constitue le symbole."*[6]

Hulme did not commit himself on the Symbolist position. Writing of Yeats, however, he said:

W. B. Yeats attempts to ennoble his craft by strenuously believing in the supernatural world, race-memory, magic and saying that symbols can recall these where prose couldn't. This is an attempt to bring in infinity again.[7]

Though he followed Bergson through proof of the existence of a reality beyond intellect, he refused to accept an easy intuition of this reality. He left Bergson at precisely the point where the French philosopher ceased to explain man's limitations and began to expound the potentialities of the

[4] *Time and Free Will,* 16.

[5] *Ibid.,* 17.

[6] Quoted by Albert Thibaudet, *La Poésie de Stéphane Mallarmé* (Paris, 1926), 110.

[7] "Notes on Language and Style," 301.

intuitive faculty; at the point, in other words, where Bergson most strikingly paralleled the philosophy of Symbolism. Hulme denied to poetry the right to deal in any way with the absolute or the unknown, insisting that the poet confine his vision to the revelation of new analogies between objects of ordinary perception. His analogies were based upon the physical because that is what man can most easily apprehend; avoiding the search for the unknown and seeking instead freshness of individual feeling, he employed imagery which had no symbolic value, and argued for a poetry that would not attempt to transcend reality but place it in new and original perspective. While he shared the Bergson-Symbolist belief in an absolute reality beyond normal perception, he firmly refused to permit introduction of this reality into his verse, and in fact established the refusal as a major premise of his poetics.

With one Symbolist, however, Hulme's aesthetic was in closer agreement. Between his notes and Remy de Gourmont's *Le Problème du style* there are curious parallels, which assume further significance as one discovers De Gourmont's authority with successive imagist poets. De Gourmont, for example, strongly emphasized the importance of the visual element in verse; in recalling a scene, he said, the artist must employ not only the emotional memory but the visual memory: *"Écrire bien, avoir style, . . . c'est peindre. . . . Sans la mémoire visuelle, sans ce réservoir d'images où puise l'imagination pour de nouvelles et infinies combinaisons, pas de style, pas de création artistique."*[8]

De Gourmont's theory rested upon an assumption that set him apart from the Symbolists of the earlier generation. He believed that the senses are the only means through

[8] *Le Problème du style* (Paris, 1907), 34, 35.

which one acquires knowledge and even explained ideas as weakened sensations.

La sensation est la base de tout, de la vie intellectuelle et morale aussi bien que de la vie physique. Deux cent cinquante ans après Hobbes, deux cent ans après Locke, telle a été la puissance destructive de Kantisme religieux, qu'on en est reduit à insister sur d'aussi élémentaires aphorismes.[9]

It follows, then, that the appeal of verse will be to the senses, and that the visual memory will deal solely with the physical object. It also follows that the poet is not a "creator"; the artistic process is a simple one in which images and fragments of images are associated in certain ways that produce a new effect.

While the resemblances to Hulme's aesthetic are striking, a fundamental divergence is just as apparent; and it is a divergence from the earlier Symbolism as well. Perhaps Hulme had read *Le Problème* and perhaps he at times echoed it, but he does not mention this source (he was not usually reticent about such matters), and, though "Cinders" was a gesture in the direction of a sensational psychology, his philosophy is in essence opposed to this theory. At the basis of Hulme's poetic, as of the early Symbolists', there is a belief in a reality beyond the material, in a knowledge not accessible to the senses; the radical difference between the theories derived from opposed views regarding the admission of reality as suitable material for the poet. Hulme, denying the poet access to it and developing a verse upon this premise, emerged with an aesthetic similar to that of De Gourmont, who for more forcible reasons had insisted

[9] *Ibid.*, 81.

upon the same denial. De Gourmont's discussion of imagery was more important for confirming the views of the later Imagists, especially Pound, who, like De Gourmont, kept aesthetics from becoming involved with the broad questions of metaphysics.

There are, however, obvious and important similarities between Hulme's imagism and Symbolism. Both called for a verse which tries to express vivid aspects of consciousness, and the reader can ignore the philosophical assumptions of Symbolism, reading *"Chanson d'Automne"* and *"Petit Air"* as, like Hulme's poems, translations into language of a condition or quality of mind or consciousness. Both are therefore intensely concerned with the techniques for expressing that which ordinarily escapes language. The Symbolist doctrine, though, with its fundamentally transcendental basis, gave poetry an authority beyond the limits Hulme had wished to establish. It was not "romantic" in exactly the sense he intended, for it accepted the discontinuity theory and faced the difficulty man encounters in trying to know the real, the barrier of language and intellect; but, by assuming the efficacy of an intuitive sense, even though it granted this power only to the poet and his art, Symbolism allowed for distortion and deprecation of the natural and objective and defined the aims of his poetry in a way Hulme believed dangerous to efficient expression. In one important respect, then, it was encumbered with ideas and terminology he attacked as romantic; and M. Taupin's generalization, in his very valuable study, that Hulme's "grain" was Symbolism is therefore somewhat misleading.

Pound was not closely acquainted with Symbolist verse until just after his *Poetry* manifesto appeared; in October, 1913, he wrote thāt he had "spent about four years puddling about on the edges of modern French poetry without getting anywhere near it."[10] He has, further, stated explicitly that "Imagisme is not symbolism";[11] and he wrote Harriet Monroe in 1913:

I think you'll find that the men in France who are seriously thinking about the ways of poetry . . . would find me fairly "sound," although I have come via a study of the ancients and the medieval writers and arrived at my beliefs without their assistance.

Yet he insisted that English poets could profit from a close study of a few French writers. And both his enthusiasm for Imagism and his conception of what it was to stand for grew, from early 1912, concurrently with his awareness of the moderns in French poetry.

His most consistent and unequivocal praise was accorded to Théophile Gautier, who did not belong to the Symbolist school—who, in fact, represented an earlier school against which Symbolism had reacted. In his *Little Review* survey of contemporary French poetry, he recommended that the reader spend some time with Gautier's two volumes before venturing upon the verse the survey was to treat. Gautier's verse, shunning vagueness, mystery, and abstraction—qualities of the romantic poetry that preceded Parnasse and of the Symbolist that followed it—met Pound's full approval. He described *Émaux et Camées* as "cut in hard substance, the shell and the Parian," and noted that the Parnassians

---

[10] "Paris," *Poetry*, Vol. III, No. 1 (October, 1913), 29-30.

[11] "Vorticism," *The Fortnightly Review*, Vol. XCVI, No. dlxxiii (September 1, 1914), 463.

had followed his advice "to cut, metaphorically, in hard stone."[12]

The clear, direct approach of *Émaux et Camées* was exactly the technique which he sought for himself. Its imagery was clear, sharply defined; Gautier, in *"L'Art,"* spoke to the poet as if he were a sculptor, or more specifically a medallion maker, working with hard materials, resistant to his will, and cutting, chiseling, these materials into figures of beauty and permanence. Difficult rhythms and stanza forms were to be his molds; colors (those of the enameller's kiln rather than water colors) and imagery of the hard, brilliant object the substance of his work. The *Émaux* were, as their title suggests, poems characterized by vivid pictorial imagery; each poem *"devait être un médaillon à enchâsser sur le couvercle d'un coffret . . . quelque chose . . . qu'on voit chez les peintres et les sculpteurs."*[13]

This is the kind of imagery one finds in Pound's Imagist poems. As he says, somewhat bitterly, in the Mauberley volume of 1920, his art (using Gautier's own words) had been an art of profile, and he had, ignoring the cheap, ephemeral standards of his time, tried for a hard, sculptured verse illustrated by the fine "Medallion" which closes the series— as if in a defiant parting gesture. Gautier's imagery also parallels that described by De Gourmont; and, except for the emphasis upon beauty, it fulfills Hulme's specifications, the image of the hard, physical object. The imagist theories of both Hulme and Pound are most closely reflected in the French poetry which differs from or ignores the metaphysical basis of Symbolism, that poetry, in other words,

[12] "The Hard and the Soft in French Poetry," *Poetry*, Vol. XI, No. 5 (February, 1918), 265, 266.
[13] *Historie du romantisme* (Paris, n.d.), 322.

which restricts the materials of art to the objective world and to reproducing, without metaphysical implications, its impact upon the observer.

After Gautier, Pound has said, France produced three chief poets: Rimbaud, Corbière, and Laforgue. Since he hardly mentioned Laforgue until 1916 or 1917, one can discount his significance for the Pound of the earlier years; but his interest in Rimbaud and Corbière began during the Imagist period. Of *"Tête de Faune,"* he wrote: It "is almost exactly the sort of beauty we are looking for now."[14] The beauty is similar to that of Gautier's poems, a surface beauty of brilliant colors: the red flowers and the faun's white teeth, the rich golds and greens of the natural background. Predominantly descriptive, the poem displays no obtrusive Symbolist intent; the poet presents his material as interesting in itself. Pound, in fact, during the 1913–17 years more or less ignored Rimbaud's avowedly Symbolist poetry; his articles devote little space to *Une Saison* or *Les Illuminations* or such poems as *"Bateau Ivre."* The visionary Rimbaud, attempting to penetrate beyond the world of external things, apparently held small interest for him.

The poems by Rimbaud which M. Taupin has cited as drawing Pound's praise belong with *"Tête de Faune."* Their subjects are slight, are taken from life around him; a cabaret in Charleroi, a casual love affair, an ugly woman emerging from her bath. The imagery is vivid but not symbolic; "Roman" pictures the sky as a little rag of somber blue, framed by a tiny branch, punctured by a star, which, little and white, dissolves in gentle shudders. What attracted Pound was craftsmanship of the kind he had discovered in

14 "The Approach to Paris," *The New Age*, Vol. XIII, No. 25 (October 16, 1913), 726.

Gautier—sharp imagery, a language at once concise and poetic, and in addition, an effort to depict clearly and realistically scenes from contemporary life. Rimbaud's poetry, like Gautier's, was both model and confirmation of Pound's modernized standards, a contemporary art he could respect. It did not, any more than Gautier's, offer examples of the specific type of image advocated by Hulme, but then Pound was not particular on this score; he was content that the Image be clear and vivid, that it convey "an intellectual and emotional complex," and he could find in Rimbaud an imagery which fulfilled these conditions.

His interest in Corbière can be briefly and similarly defined, though neither he nor Taupin makes such illuminating reference to specific poems as one finds in the comment on *"Tête de Faune."* Pound thought Corbière significant for his style, or rather, for the liberties he took with it.

He was as careless of style as a man of swift mordant speech can be. For the quintessence of style is precisely that it should be swift and mordant. It is precisely that a man should not speak at all until he has something (it matters very little what) to say.[15]

The words might have been written with his own "The Temperaments" or other of his epigrammatic poems in mind. Again, he admired Corbière for the same quality he had found in Gautier, the same which he desired for his own verse, the quality of hardness. For Pound, the French poets were an inspiration, a confirmation, but not a source of theory. He admired their technical proficiency, but he was uninterested in the philosophy of Symbolism, and he

[15] "The Approach to Paris," *The New Age*, Vol. XIII, No. 23 (October 2, 1913), 664.

ignored those poets and that verse which most closely approximated a Symbolist pattern.

The relation of the theory stated in the 1915–16 anthologies, "Amygism," to the Symbolist aesthetic is somewhat more ambiguous. In 1915, Remy de Gourmont wrote:

Les imagistes anglais precèdent évidemment des symbolistes français. On voit cela tout d'abord à leur horreur du cliché, l'horreur de la rhétorique et du grandiose, du genre oratoire, genre facile dont les imitateurs de Victor Hugo . . . nous ont dégoûtés à jamais. Comme préceptes positifs, ils veulent la précision du langage, la netteté de la vision, la concentration de la pensée qu'ils aiment à synthétiser dans une image dominante.[16]

Aldington quoted the passage in an article for the *Bruno Chap Books;* Amy Lowell used it to introduce an account of the movement for *Poetry;* and their preface to *Some Imagist Poets* (1916) incorporated it into an Imagist manifesto. They were obviously willing to permit belief in a fundamental similarity between the two aesthetics.

The similarity does not entirely hold for Hulme and Pound, and one suspects it was not really intended to hold for the theory of the later group. Association with Symbolism, a well-established school, was to their advantage, whether or not it was actually warranted by the facts. Aldington would only allow that the Imagists tolerated Symbolism; Amy Lowell spoke more generally but to the same end. Her distinction between the attitudes she described as *internality* and *externality* and her disapproval of the former place her at odds with the broad philo-

[16] *"Revue du Mois," Mercure de France,* Vol. CXI (May-August, 1915), 355.

sophical element in the Symbolist aesthetic. *Externality,* the Imagist and modern attitude, cuts the poet away from introspection and focuses his attention upon the object as interesting for itself alone. While she does not directly attack the Symbolists' transcendental view of external reality, she unquestionably condemns it by inference. The line of demarcation is clear: the poet could hold, with Hulme and the Imagists, that his art should be confined to the precise, external, physical world, or, with the early Symbolists, that it should be an attempt to penetrate the external to the vague and shadowy life beyond; he could deal strictly with man's sensitivity to and imaginative awareness of the external world, or he could use the external and man's consciousness as the basis for something beyond either.

Both, of course, transcend a purely mechanical view of art (cf. Hulme's "visual chord," Pound's Image, and the Symbolist theory that the finished work contains the quality of the living or the real) and use the resources of language to convey a feeling more or less complex, more or less difficult to define—and the Imagist poem is just as much a symbol of a feeling as the Symbolist poem. The Imagist could admire and emulate the Symbolists' aim of establishing poetry as a medium separate and distinguishable from any other (which may partially account for the "romantic" tone of Symbolist theory); he could even claim, as Flint reported, that poetry is all science, all religion, all philosophy and metaphysics (though he meant this as a statement of value rather than of fact); he could study and admire Symbolist technique, especially in the work of the younger poets, like De Gourmont, who abandoned philosophical idealism as unnecessary and irrelevant to artistic idealism. But he was suspicious of Symbolism so far as it became involved with metaphysics, transforming the sensations received from the objective world into perceptions of Truth or a Reality dependent upon, but above, art.

This ambivalent reaction to Symbolism also throws some light upon the Imagist's relationship to his immediate predecessors in English poetry. The poets of the nineties, too, had found Symbolism interesting and had translated Symbolist verse (Symons' book on the French school, in fact, serving the Imagists as a way into Symbolism). But they were attracted by characteristics that the Imagists ignored: a vagueness which follows upon the belief that poetry offers a mystic's escape from actuality, a refusal to deal directly with the real and concrete and a withdrawal into a diffuse but pervasive melancholy, a use of words (for their sounds and colors) to suggest an essence beyond the object for which they stand—all of which marked the romanticism of the late nineteenth century in English poetry. While the Imagists carry on certain of the principles of the nineties—insistence upon intensity of feeling (and therefore a kind of subjectivity), denial of values other than those of art, and (in some cases) an emphasis upon beauty—their attitude toward poetry avoids the earlier romantic posturings and returns to exact consideration of the external world. That they often failed to go much beyond the details or data of this world is partially explained by their concentration upon rejecting or breaking up the old forms of verse and bringing its language once again close to what gives it distinctness of definition.

Imagist theories of verse rhythms clearly echo those of the Symbolists; from Hulme to Amy Lowell, their theory and practice developed from models they found in contemporary French literature. Hulme, widely read in Symbolist verse, pointed to Gustave Kahn's statement of the principles of *vers libre* as the primary cause of the contemporary renaissance in French poetry, and called upon English poets to establish new forms for their verse if they would see a similar revival in their own country. He was not, however, able to offer them any constructive advice beyond the assertion that Imagism did "not require the old metric system," and beyond the example of his own practice: lines, loosely iambic, of irregular length. His principal interest lay elsewhere, and, content to suggest the French poets as models, he was himself unable to progress beyond the *libre* aspect of *vers libre*.

While Kahn has been given credit for inventing the new form, and while he was Hulme's chief source, he was less well known to Pound and to the other Imagists, who looked instead to certain of his followers. In 1910, Charles Vildrac and Georges Duhamel had published their *Notes sur la technique poétique*, a defense of *vers libre*. Two years later, Vildrac was invited to speak in London and delivered three lectures on modern French poetry; Flint attended the lectures and perhaps Pound, who had previously met Vildrac in Paris, and Aldington were also present. Both Flint and Pound refer specifically to the *Notes* in their correspondence or in published or unpublished articles.

The goal of Vildrac and Duhamel was flexibility of metre, but not complete freedom from the demands of metrical form. They merely hoped to furnish poets with a means of breaking the rigidity of the Alexandrine, the traditional French line. Their proposal, for which they acknowledged their indebtedness to Kahn, was a line whose length would be determined by natural definition into units of speech or of thought, rather than an arbitrary definition into a predetermined syllable count. Quoting Kahn, they said: *"L'unité du vers peut se définir: Un fragment le plus court possible figurant un arrêt de voix et un arrêt de sens."*[17]

At the same time, recognizing the need for pattern, which such a determination might well not offer, they suggested that each line ought to contain an element called the *rhythmic constant*. Always composed of the same number of syllables, the constant was to give the poem the repetitive effect necessary to unified pattern. It was a means of admitting the value of metre without forcing all other elements of the poem to give way before it: regular or traditional verse consists entirely of constants; free verse of a constant and an additional unit that varies with the demands set up by content and the limitations of the speaking voice. In the following verses the unitalicized five-syllable phrase is the rhythmic constant.

> *Il y a une armoire* à peine luisante,
> Qui a entendu *les voix de mes grand'tantes,*
> Qui a entendu *la voix de mon grand-père,*
> Qui a entendu *la voix de mon père.*
> A ses souvenirs *l'armoire est fidèle*
> On a tort de croir(e) *qu'elle ne sait que se taire . . . .*[18]

This is clearly not free, in the sense of formless, verse; its rhythmical form is achieved by means comparable with those Whitman often used (cf. the opening lines of "Out of the Cradle"). Vildrac and Duhamel insisted that the listener or reader should have no doubt regarding interpretation of the poet's rhythm; as another contemporary wrote:

[17] *Notes sur la technique poétique* (Paris, 1925), 7.
[18] *Ibid.*, 15–16.

"Il n'y a pas de poésie sans rhythme, ni de rhythme sans nombre."[19] They believed verse the result of strict and clear demands of feeling and meaning; the poet who dedicated himself to literally free verse was in danger of not writing verse at all. Besides the constant, they recommended other devices for the establishment of pattern and unity: proportional arrangement of units within a line, alliteration, assonance, and even occasional rhyme.

The theory of Kahn and of the *Notes* had no necessary relation to the use of the symbol. It was only another sign of the general feeling that the metric of poetry needed overhauling to accommodate the new subject matter poetry was called upon to express. Symbolists like Francis Vielé-Griffin, Émile Verhaeren, and Francis Jammes made conscious use of *vers libre,* but except that they adapted traditional rhythms to heighten the feeling of mystery, the masters of Symbolism were not *vers libristes.* Free verse was, in fact, even less obviously related to Symbolism than it was to the imagism of Hulme's theory. Although Hulme insisted that he did not recommend *vers libre,* the new metric was a reasonable and useful concomitant of his imagism, not so much because of its musical effects as because it allowed wider choice of language.

Pound had already established for himself a background in the composition of free forms before he began close study of Symbolist poetry. He had a wide knowledge of prosody other than English and borrowed freely where it suited his needs; he wrote to Williams in 1908: "Sometimes I use rules of Spanish, Anglo-Saxon, and Greek metric that are not common in the English of Milton's or Miss Austen's day." When he published his manifesto in *Poetry,* he in-

[19] De Gourmont, *Le Problème du style,* 171.

sisted upon the importance of freedom from overbearing demands of English prosody; the Imagists wrote, he said, in sequence of the musical phrase rather than sequence of the metronome.

He admittedly borrowed from the French the term *vers libre*, which began to appear in his criticism soon after Imagism was made public; as his authority on the subject he cited the Vildrac-Duhamel book. But his concept of free verse never became a copy of the French, the difference lying partly in his rejection of the rhythmic constant or return and partly in his emphasis upon a quantitative measure that the French language does not permit.[20] His closest and most consistent model or ideal was not poetry at all, but music; while his line was determined, as was the French, by the limitations of meaning and of the speaking voice, rather than by a preconceived metre, he built his patterns upon his own standards of appropriateness; he combined words into phrases as a musician combines notes into phrases, according to the harmony deriving from the pitch and duration of their sounds, or at least he did so to the extent permitted by the demands of the sense. At its best, his metric may be seen in "Δώρία."

> *Be in me as the eternal moods*
> *of the bleak wind, and not*
> *As transient things are—*
> *gaiety of flowers.*

[20] One should note, however, his early emphatic admiration of the rhythms of De Gourmont's *Livres des Litanies*; see "The Approach to Paris," *The New Age*, Vol. XIII, No. 20 (September 11, 1913), 518. René Taupin, *L'Influence du symbolisme français sur la poésie Américaine (de 1910 à 1920)* (Paris, 1929), 137, suggests that Pound's "The Alchemist" owes something to the *Litanies;* but this poem seems to have been written before Pound was closely acquainted with French poetry.

Although the lines, unavoidably, pull toward the accentual, this element is as carefully modulated as is possible in English. Measured by stress, the metre is chaotic; measured by standards which consider pitch, assonance, and quantity, it has an ordered, melodic quality that certainly brings poetry close to music.

A word about Eliot's early views on free verse may be relevant. They differed from those of Pound, but the two reached an agreement by 1917 that some step needed to be taken as a counter to abuses of the *vers libre* they were doing much to popularize. Eliot never succumbed to the tendency to write a verse completely free of the traditional metrical schemes. He experimented with the blank verse of Webster and the early seventeenth-century dramatists, as Laforgue had done with traditional French measures; instead of seeking complete freedom, he recommended establishment of a simple norm like iambic pentameter and then constantly withdrawing from it, or suggestion of a norm by constant approximation to one. Thus he and Pound held distinctly different views on the nature of English free verse, a fact upon which each has commented; but they concurred upon Eliot's statement in 1917 that "*Vers libre* does not exist, and it is time that this preposterous fiction followed the *élan vital* and the eighty thousand Russians into oblivion. . . . There is no escape from metre; there is only mastery."[21] As a corrective for the abuse of freedom, they turned to the tight quatrain of the Parnassian Gautier, the metric of the Sweeney poems and of certain sections of the Mauberley series.

With the prefaces to the anthologies of 1915 and 1916, *vers libre* became an official adjunct to Imagism. For Aldington, Amy Lowell, and Fletcher, free verse, rather than the image or the symbol, was the attraction of French poetry; and only Amy Lowell had not written in some free form before acquaintance with the French poets. Aldington has said:

> I began to write vers libre about the early part of 1911, partly because I was fatigued with rhyme and partly because of the interest I had in poetic experiment. I . . . never suspected the existence of the French vers libristes. I got the idea from a chorus in the Hippolytus of Euripides.

Once exposed to French theory, however, he quickly adapted the systematic exposition of a free form to his own purposes. He borrowed the term *rhythmic constant,* whose length and regularity of appearance he made the standard for distinguishing between verse and prose; and his interpretation of Imagism described its free verse in the language of Vildrac and Duhamel. The fourth principle was "individuality of rhythm. We make new fashions instead of cutting our clothes on the old models. Mr. Hueffer says that the unit of our rhythms is the unit of conversation. I daresay he is right."[22]

The unit of rhythm in his early poems is unquestionably the unit of conversation, the lines terminating with a voice and a sense stop, but his reliance upon a constant to unify a poem is not so easily discernible. Yvor Winters has studied Aldington's "Choricos" and decided that in it one

[21] "Reflections on Vers Libre," *The New Statesman,* Vol. VIII, No. 204 (March 3, 1917), 518, 519. It is interesting to note that Eliot's *"Le Directeur"* followed a free-verse pattern which is described by Vildrac and Duhamel in *Notes,* 27.

[22] "Modern Poetry and the Imagists," *The Egoist,* Vol. I, No. 11 (June 1, 1914), 203.

finds a recurrence of both traditional feet (lines 1–4) and a single-accent free-verse foot (lines 3–7). Beyond the first seven lines, Mr. Winters can find no pattern, and certainly there appears no single rhythmical factor, for almost half the lines of the poem do not conform to any of the usual schemes. At the same time, "Choricos" is far from lacking completely in the devices Aldington recommended, though the devices are varied. For example, nearly one-third of the lines begin with an anapestic foot, whose movement is retarded by frequent use of unaccented syllables whose quantitative value approximates that of the accented syllable. It is also evident that groups of lines at least are unified by a pattern of initial reiteration which has the effect of a constant. These devices are used with some frequency through the poem, and though they do not give a single unity, they give cohesiveness enough to avoid violation of the poem's clear unity of feeling.

Other poems show a similarly free expression. "To a Greek Marble" opens with four lines in a traditional pattern. From these carefully measured lines, it proceeds to others that have no immediately recognizable measure, but nevertheless show a kind of organization, stanza 2 being based upon a principle of balance between lines 5 and 6 and lines 7 and 8, with a ninth line which, repeated at the close of the poem, has the effect of a refrain. "At Mitylene" uses certain of the devices of Biblical prose, its lines held together by co-ordination of sentence units and by repetition of the words in these units which emphasize their parallel structure. The rhythms of these poems avoid the formal metrical schemes, and their freedom is greater even than that advised by Vildrac and Duhamel.

Amy Lowell preferred to call *vers libre* by Flint's term,

unrhymed cadence, and, after her French mentors, she described it as built upon " 'organic rhythm,' or the rhythm of the speaking voice with its necessity for breathing, rather than on a strict metrical system."[23] She also borrowed the concept of the return, though she put it to a different use: "The rhythm of prose is long and slightly curved, the rhythm of verse is much shorter, with a tendency to return back upon itself."[24] However, she was satisfied neither with the mere statement of these concepts nor with a hit-or-miss method of experimenting with them; through a series of experiments with Mr. Patterson of Columbia University, she set about to put them on a reasonable and, if possible, scientific basis. She read her "Thompson's Lunch Room" and H. D.'s "Oread" into Patterson's "sound photographing machine," and after several rereadings and a study of results felt that she could confidently assert as proved two theories about unrhymed cadence: that cadence represents "a line rising to a certain height and then dropping away to mount again, farther on";[25] that a poem in free verse may achieve the effect of the return by the recurrence of one particular time-length between accents. Ignoring the question of line measurement, she here concentrated upon the time unit between primary accents as the organizing factor in free verse, and her analysis explained the normative "foot" in these terms rather than in the terms of a syllable count, as in French, or of a fixed count of stressed and unstressed syllables, as in English. Perhaps she was also dem-

[23] *Sword Blades and Poppy Seeds* (Boston and New York, 1914), *xi.*
[24] "Vers Libre and Metrical Prose," *Poetry,* Vol. III, No. 6 (March, 1914), 214.
[25] "The Rhythms of Free Verse," *The Dial,* Vol. LXIV, No. 758 (January 17, 1918), 52.

onstrating, after the fact, that strong feeling, given adequate expression, will automatically assume a pattern.[26]

Her polyphonic prose is relevant to Imagism only as another instance of borrowing and adaptation from French poets. An oratorical prose, it employed assonance, alliteration, rhyme, and "return." The Imagists balked at it, but she won her argument for including some of it in an anthology and even converted Fletcher to her practice. Her experiments, however, are less important for establishing firm guidance to those who wished freer forms than for the vigor with which she espoused the cause of freedom. Interested in poetry as a spoken art, she was able, by the force of her personality, to shift attention from the image and to link Imagism so prominently with the battle over *vers libre* that what was presumably its central doctrine lost much of its significance. French poetry, providing her with models, thus was to a great extent responsible for this change in the nature of Imagist doctrine.

Fletcher, in fact, could claim a belief in free verse as his only tie to the Imagists. He made some experiments in free verse before he studied French poetry, his principal model being Whitman, "who seems the only poet who gave my sort of impression of the modern city." In 1909, he wrote some verse patterned after Whitman, but he returned the next year to the traditional forms. Extensive reading in the French poets soon drew him back toward the freer rhythms, and by 1912 he was convinced that such radical experiment was a necessity to the art of his generation.

Like Pound, he was interested in the quantitative aspects

[26] Cf. De Gourmont, *Le Problème du style*, 171, on the necessity in free verse that there be a line which recurs at almost regular intervals and thus reassures and guides the ear.

of rhythm and emphasized the parallels between poetry and music. He developed from these convictions a belief in the need for a free form of verse, and, having become acquainted with the French *vers libre* theorists, had recourse to their justification of freedom: "Each line of a poem, however many or few its stresses, represents a single breath, and therefore a single perception."[27] Fletcher stated the difference between poetry and prose in terms of general psychological effect: in prose, there is a direct, orderly progression from point to point of a flat surface; sentences in developing this point move on and do not return upon themselves.

In poetry, we have a succession of curves. The direction of the thought is not in straight lines, but wavy and spiral. It rises and falls on gusts of strong emotion. Most often it creates strongly marked loops and spirals.[28]

Rhyme and metre may help to emphasize these loops and circles, but have nothing essential to do with poetry; they merely reproduce patterns which would be better reproduced through freer expression of the artist's emotion.

With this statement one arrives at an extreme to which the English and American *vers libristes* had gone in their demands for freedom. It illustrates the dangers that accompanied establishment of a model from another language with a different prosody. Fletcher's theory, of which there is at least an echo in Amy Lowell's, has drawn free verse almost to the assumption made by Whitman: that poetic content would of itself produce poetic form. The difficulties

[27] *Irradiations: Sand and Spray* (Boston and New York, 1915), Preface, *xii.*
[28] *Goblins and Pagodas* (Boston and New York, 1916), Preface, *xii.*

experienced by the English poets in discovering in their language as unifying a basis for free verse as the French had found in theirs have been suggested in the passages on Aldington and Amy Lowell; confronted with such difficulties, it would appear that the poet might tend to take the easier way of rejecting *any* preconceived pattern and hoping that the emotion, accurately and fully expressed, would produce its own characteristic, pleasing, and appropriate rhythm. Practice among the Imagists varied; Eliot has said that there were three kinds of free verse: his (accentual, approximating the iambic line), Pound's (quantitative, taking account of word sounds in certain combinations), and Whitman's (that which is ostensibly free of accentual or quantitative norms and establishes its pattern by other means). Imagism included all three in its effort to break up traditional forms by re-examining the poetic line as well as the poetic image.

Even in theories of metric, Imagist and Symbolist sought a more expressive and a more personal idiom, which suggests a final comment on the relationship between the two doctrines. They withdrew into the subjective and personal, though claiming objectivity on the basis of precise technique; the Imagist, however, by employing image rather than symbol, seems to achieve greater objectivity and at the same time to restrict much more narrowly the limits of poetry. He also avoids the obscurity with which the Symbolists were charged (cf. the attitudes of Mallarmé that a degree of *énigme* is inevitable, of De Gourmont that clarity of thought is not an essential quality of poetry and that art is, by its disinterestedness, absolutely unintelligible to the masses of people); but Imagism, in its time, was also criticized on this ground, for the feelings and sensations of the

Imagists were sometimes difficult for the reader to understand. And by its accomplishment in making French theory and poetry known to English and American poets, Imagism is to a certain extent responsible for the attitude towards obscurity which has influenced the poetry that followed it. The Imagist, in fact, found De Gourmont's statement and attitude sympathetic; and, again according to Flint's (and Pound's) report on the school in *Poetry*, admitted to a degree of *snobisme* himself.

V

Lesser and Greater Lights

ALTHOUGH the theory of Hulme has claimed the major share of attention, three other poets were also, at one time or another, in a position to have influenced the doctrines of Imagism. Edward Storer, for example, was a member of both clubs founded by Hulme, and Flint has testified that he led the 1909 group in discussions of the image. Flint himself not only belonged to both clubs but contributed to all four of the Imagist anthologies. Ford Madox Hueffer discovered Lawrence and published early writing by Pound and Aldington. He regularly entertained the Imagists at his lodgings, and one of his poems was included in their first anthology. Storer was not widely known before Imagism began, but Flint had won some prominence, and Hueffer's position as a reputable editor and critic was well established. Might not the theories of these three have had some influence in shaping Imagist doctrine?

The case for Storer rests upon his membership in the poetry clubs and upon two statements by Flint. The first suggests that he, more aggressively than Hulme, directed attention to the image in poetry; the second classes him with Hulme as an early experimenter in Imagist technique: "There is no difference, except that which springs from difference of temperament and talent, between an Imagist poem of today and those written by Edward Storer and T. E. Hulme."[1] Flint has recently qualified these remarks from the 1915 "History," asserting that Storer's concept of the image was different from the one expounded by Hulme.

Moreover, what little interest Storer took in the movement seems to have been professional rather than paternal. Aldington commissioned him to translate the *Poems and Fragments of Sappho* and the *Rustic Letters* of Aelianus for *The Egoist's* Poets' Translation Series. In his turn, Storer wrote a review of the 1915 anthology which he published in *The British Review*, though his attitude toward the book failed to satisfy at least one of the Imagists. He further secured for Aldington a letter of introduction to the editor of the magazine in the vain hope of opening its pages to Imagist poems. Otherwise, Storer and the Imagists were evidently not interested in each other.

Storer's definition of poetry marks him as inclining toward the Symbolist rather than the Hulme concept:

It is mystery, reserve, control which are the attraction in letters as well as in life. . . . True poetry . . . is like true and great love in this, that in its supreme expression it speaks really for the race rather than for the individual.[2]

In 1908, the preface to his *Mirrors of Illusion* had attacked traditional metrics, and he consistently favored a free verse form, though by 1916 he admitted *vers libre* to be a "literary

[1] "The History of Imagism," *The Egoist*, Vol. II, No. 5 (May 1, 1915), 70–71.
[2] "Two Women Poets," *The English Review*, Vol. V (May, 1910), 189.

expression which has failed to take its most convenient and final shape." He was less vocal about whatever theories he may have held regarding imagery; but the imagery of his early poems has little in common with that advocated by Hulme. It is descriptive rather than analogical in method, the picture conveys an emotion by itself without reliance upon analogy. And it is suggestive rather than expressive, to use the distinction drawn by Bergson. The method and subject matter are strongly reminiscent of Symbolist poetry, and it was as a Symbolist (and a romantic) that Storer was classed by Flint. "I see romanticism behind footlights; symbolism as a sharp sword of light stretching through darkness."[3] However prominently he may have figured in the conversations of the 1909 club, it is clear that he and Hulme were not discussing the same kind of image. His attitude toward the movement and the attitude of its members toward him reduce the chances that his work may in any way have influenced its doctrine. Pound minimized his importance; Fletcher dismissed him as "simply an aesthete of the nineties."

In his *Annals of Innocence and Experience*, Herbert Read says that F. S. Flint had more to do with Imagism than has been acknowledged, and as one examines Flint's accomplishments between 1908–17, the justice of the remark becomes increasingly apparent. A protégé of A. R. Orage, he was given the duties of verse reviewer for *The New Age* and as early as 1908 had the opportunity to explain his poetic theory in the pages of a respected journal. He made the most of his good fortune and produced a column which was not content to post notices of new books but judged them according to carefully defined, though

[3] "Verse," *The New Age*, Vol. VI, No. 6 (December 9, 1909), 137.

unabstruse, critical standards. If for no other reason than his early prominence in the Imagist scene, Flint must be considered as a possible influence on its doctrine.

His eloquent efforts to reawaken interest in modern poetry were badly needed in 1908. He deplored the absence from contemporary verse of the lively activity which brings new poets.

English poetry at this hour is deliquescent. There is no unity of inspiration; the little winds blow fitfully in all directions; and no criticism. There can be no movement, therefore . . . although I believe we have the timber to build the ships with.[4]

The pervading theme of his column was exhortation to modern writers to bring English poetry out of the doldrums. Time and again he stated his belief in the need for a "revaluation of all poetical values."

Old England is senile, and poetry lacks criticism and ideas; perhaps England may one day cast her skin, like the snake, and poetry acquire freshness again. . . . Every artist sloughs at least one skin. Let him then slough England's senility and sloth, and perhaps recreate England in the process.[5]

Believing that every generation must find its own poetic formula, he reproached the moderns for imitating the formulas of other ages. He demanded that poets take stock of their ideas, reject those inappropriate to the conditions of modern life, and formulate a new theory.

At the same time, he offered what he considered a suit-

4 "Verse," *The New Age*, Vol. V, No. 14 (August 5, 1909), 288–89.
5 "Verse," *The New Age*, Vol. VI, No. 14 (February 3, 1910), 327.

able, modern definition of poetry. Poetry, he said, is the result of "art directing the emotions and moving in a dream; and Nature, as Oscar Wilde has said, and as Scott proved, is a bore. She only provides beauty with the ornaments that set off or suggest the intensity of the vision."[6] The importance of his definition lies in its overtones rather than in its imprecise denotation. It recalls Flint's intense admiration for the poetry of his French contemporaries. As he discussed the French poets, praising them for the sincere inspiration and meticulous technique he hoped to encourage among his English readers, he revealed his fundamental sympathy for a symbolist concept of poetry.

The Romantics were content to tell a story, the Parnassians impassably to describe; but the Symbolist—and all essential poets are symbolists—takes a pure emotion and translates it by eternal images which become symbolical of man's everlasting desires and questionings. . . . It is true that the French avowed symbolist poets went astray in their discontent and wrote hermetical verse in which the sense and appeal were completely occulted; but these too were only experiments.[7]

Through his reviews Flint elaborated other aspects of his poetic theory. His first *New Age* column argued that the "day of the lengthy poem is over—at least, for this troubled age. . . . The long poem is, I believe, an historical error."[8] Among the first to appreciate the beauty of Japanese verse, which was just then beginning to appear in trans-

[6] "Book of the Week," *The New Age*, Vol. IV, No. 9 (December 24, 1908), 185.

[7] "Verse," *The New Age*, Vol. V, No. 23 (September 30, 1909), 413.

[8] "Recent Verse,"*The New Age*, Vol. VII, No. 11 (July 11, 1908), 213; "Book of the Week," *ibid.*, Vol. III, No. 16 (August 15, 1908), 312.

lation, he pointed to this poetry as proof of the artistic effects obtainable from "brief fragments" rather than long poems. His judgment on metrical form was not delivered so quickly. While he voiced his desire for greater freedom of expression than traditional patterns permit, he hesitated to accept completely the obvious answer offered by the French poets whose verse he manifestly respected. He wrote in 1908: "it is to be feared . . . that the new humanity will prefer more subtle rhythms and broken cadences."[9] But he also expressed dissatisfaction with a volume of verse because its author had not provided the traditional rhyme, and, in reviewing Pound's *Personae*, suggested that a free form of verse might lead a poet "into the wastes." However, he gradually became absorbed in the rhythmical aspects of poetry: "I have defined in these columns great poetry as great rhythm, rhythm of idea and rhythm of execution";[10] and he turned without qualification to *vers libre* as encouraging the full communication of the poetic impulse:

The old devices of regular metrical beat and regular rhyming are worn out; the sonnet and the three-quatrain poem will probably always live; but for the larger music verse must be free from all restraints of a regular rhythm and a squared-up frame; the poet must forge his rhythm according to the impulse of the creative emotion working through him.[11]

Specifically, Flint recommended that the poet employ what he called *unrhymed cadence*, his name for free verse.

[9] "Recent Verse," *The New Age*, Vol. III, No. 11 (July 11, 1908), 213.

[10] "The Sovereign Rhythms," *The New Age*, Vol. VII, No. 21 (September 22, 1910), 497.

[11] "Reviews," *The New Age*, Vol. VI, No. 10 (January 6, 1910), 234.

He called it *cadence* rather than *vers libre* because the new word avoided the connotation of metrical regularity associated with the word *verse*. He hoped, in fact, to divorce poetry from its hitherto inevitable association with measure.

There is no difference of kind between prose and verse. Since they are both words in order, and both have rhythm, it is obvious that they are essentially the same. Verse, however, has measure as well as rhythm. It may also have rhyme, "Free verse" has no measure, and it cannot, therefore, properly be called "verse." "Cadence" would be a better word for it. Cadence differs in no way from prose. Its rhythm is more strongly felt, and it is printed in lines of varying length in order that this rhythm may be marked. But there is no justification for printing prose in this way, except to point to a definite rhythmic intention.[12]

The application of Flint's theory may be seen in the poem "Trees," which appeared in *Some Imagist Poets* (1915). The lines cannot be measured into traditional feet; and no line recurs with sufficient regularity to be accepted as the basic metrical or rhythmic unit of the poem—although the initial line of each stanza, naming a tree, provides the suggestion of pattern, and each stanza develops from this first, short, heavily accented line. Within the stanzas, the lines, which are phrases or grammatical units, tend to lengthen in the middle of each stanza and then grow shorter toward the close; the stanzas, by variations in length, also hint of a cadence or overall rhythm, although the poem is probably too brief for this device to operate with any appreciable effect.

[12] "Presentation .·. . ," *The Chap Book*, Vol. II, No. 9 (March, 1920), 18.

This is not precisely the concept of the French *vers libristes*, but it is clear that Flint felt he was borrowing from them or at least adapting their ideas to English prosody. He does not mention Kahn, although his comprehensive knowledge of French poetry must have brought him in touch with Kahn's ideas; but there can be no doubt that he knew the theories of Duhamel and Vildrac. He heard Vildrac's lectures in London; and he cited their *Notes* in a criticism of Amy Lowell's metrical conservatism.

Flint's Imagist poems show little deviation from the fundamentals of his theory. They are written in unrhymed cadence like that of his "Trees." Occasionally one finds a clear, sharp image which pictures a natural object so distinctly that it draws the reader's notice and is interesting in itself.

The sunlight gilds the tops
of the poplar spires, far off,
behind the houses.[13]

Or one discovers a striking metaphor which translates the poetic into ordinary, mundane terms, evidence that Flint had read or heard Hulme with some profit.

On black bare trees a stale cream moon
hangs dead, and sours the unborn buds.[14]

But instances of the Hulme technique are scarce.[15] In Flint's

[13] "Cones," *Some Imagist Poets* (Boston, 1916), 56.
[14] "Eau-Forte," *Some Imagist Poets* (1915), 63.
[15] That Flint had heard Hulme with profit is suggested by the following lines from "Presentation," p. 19: "Metaphor has been called the creation of new words, and the originality of a poet has been held to be comparable to his power of making metaphors. The language is strewn with dead metaphors."

poems, the image usually is a more or less conventional symbol, a natural object selected because it symbolizes a feeling experienced by the poet. In "Fragment" there is a series of rather conventional images, each of which helps suggest the feeling the poet has for the women to whom he speaks. "The Swan," a better poem, is dominated by a single symbol. The first stanza, with some skill, establishes the lush, natural scene in which the swan will appear; the second shifts in tone, as the swan is first mentioned, with the use of images of the cold and hard object; the third transforms the swan into a symbol of a special kind of beauty whose presence tempers the poet's sorrow. The descriptive technique of stanzas 1 and 2 is consistent with Imagist practice, but the intent of stanza 3 is not; even had he, as Hulme would have recommended, eliminated the reference to *sorrow* (thus, perhaps, improving his poem), his purpose would have extended beyond the implicit, and sometimes explicit, purpose of Imagist doctrine.

Consistent with his criticism of the French Symbolists, Flint avoids obscurity: the swan clearly symbolizes beauty, its progress beauty's effect upon sorrow. Flint is trying to communicate an idea much less complex than Mallarmé tried when he dealt with the same symbol. Mallarmé sought to embody in his poem a feeling for the unreality of the abstract; Flint sought to give the abstract a clear objectification. Nevertheless, in avoiding obscurity he frequently failed to avoid the alternate danger of becoming conventional; while he sought to objectify an emotion, he frequently did not make the intellectual effort necessary to give the emotion aesthetic significance. Perhaps the adequate symbol can provide expression as exact as the analogy Hulme recommended; but in many cases Flint did not find the adequate symbol and departed from objectivity as his feelings and personality overflowed into the poem. On occasion he relaxed his control to the extent of stating a feeling directly, as he did in the poem "Easter," which closes on an anti-climatic line of personal comment.

As a source of Imagism, Flint is on the side of Symbolism and the early poetry of Edward Storer. Unlike Storer, he joined the Imagist movement soon after its inception, was respected by its members, and may have had some influence in shaping its theory, if only by acquainting the Imagists with French poetry. Unlike the Symbolists, he recommended that the poet strive for clarity in his presentation. On this score, his theory approaches Hulme's; but he was none the less a symbolist rather than an Imagist poet. He did not believe in restricting poetry to the material or the external world, and he saw no particular importance in the use of striking analogy; his principal contribution was his demand for a fresh vigor in poetry—a freshness to be achieved mainly through new rhythmical forms.

Ford Madox Hueffer's claims to attention are stronger than Flint's, though his relationship to Imagism has in the main gone unnoticed. One need look no farther than Hueffer himself for an unqualified statement of his importance to the movement. In 1914, Hueffer declared to Aldington that he was after all the only real Imagist and that all its doctrines were derived from him. In 1930 he repeated his claims, though less confidently. He hoped that Imagism might have profited by its acquaintance with three of his theories: the word has energies which transcend its sounds or letters; emotions have their own proper cadence; poetic ideas are best expressed by the rendering of concrete objects.

It is evident that the Imagists respected his work. Aldington complimented Harriet Monroe for her acceptance of "On Heaven," saying he felt that Hueffer's artistry in this poem had put them all, even Yeats, to shame. When Hueffer's *Collected Poems* appeared in 1913, Pound reviewed it for *The New Freewoman* as "the most important book of the season";[16] thirty years later he wrote to William Carlos Williams: "I did Fordie as much justice as anyone (or almost anyone) did—but still not enough! . . . Fordie knew more about writing than any of 'them' or of 'us.' "

To describe Hueffer's literary technique, his contemporaries borrowed a term from the vocabulary of art: they called him an Impressionist. Since it was fashionable at the time to be an *-ist* of one kind or another, Hueffer accepted the judgment without cavil and graciously explained his understanding of the Impressionist method in literature. Fundamentally "the Impressionist gives you himself, how he reacts to a fact; not the fact itself; or rather, not so much the fact itself. . . . Impressionism is a frank expression of personality."[17] This does not mean, however, that the artist allows his personality to intrude upon his work. For example, he does not preach or moralize; he communicates his view of life as it is, not as he would like it to be. Nor does he offer the reader the bare, uninterpreted fact, but through intellectual effort transforms the fact into an imaginative communication. Quoting Stephen Crane, Hueffer warned: "You must render: never report." Never say: "He saw a man aim a gun at him"; but: "He saw a steel ring directed

[16] "Ford Madox Hueffer," *The New Freewoman*, Vol. 1, No. 13 (December 15, 1913), 251.
[17] "On Impressionism," *Poetry and Drama*, Vol. II, No. 2 (June, 1914), 175.

at him."[18] Never say, "I am happy!"; but simply act as if you *are* happy.[19]

In other words, the Impressionist tries to record, in objective terms, his "impression of a moment." In order to illustrate further, Hueffer referred to the paintings of the Futurists, who "are only trying to render on canvas what Impressionists *tel que moi* have been trying to render for many years." The Futurist painter expressing his view of "A Night Out" might produce a canvas picturing in one corner a pair of stays; in another, a fragment of an early morning landscape; in the middle, a pair of eyes. While he makes no direct statement, he obviously conveys the essential elements of the night, the impression of it that remains to him. Equally important, he has given the impression an objective character, has given it a hardness which should be a component quality of all works of art.[20]

Hueffer believed Impressionism to be an inevitable refuge for the contemporary artist. Modern life has become so complex, the limits of knowledge have been so expanded, that no one man can hope to comprehend more than segments of it. "Nowadays we may contemplate life steadily enough, but it is impossible to see it whole."[21] Until all of the sciences have been so "crystallized" by specialists that the individual may again be able to understand them, poetry "of the great manner" will be impossible. Meanwhile, the poet must be content to restrict his attention to the small areas which he can know; he must be introspective and

[18] "Techniques," *The Southern Review*, Vol. I, No. 1 (July, 1935), 31.

[19] Preface, *Imagist Anthology* (New York, 1930), 19.

[20] "On Impressionism," *Poetry and Drama*, Vol. II, No. 2 (June, 1914), 182.

[21] *The Critical Attitude* (London, 1915), 28.

render his own impressions and moods; in this way he may contribute to the science of human nature, which is the proper sphere of the arts.

We are approaching, in fact, once more to a state such as that which produced ballads and folk-songs. . . . Ballads and folk-songs are never Great Poetry, but what exquisite pleasure they can give us, and what a light they can throw upon the human heart! And that, in essence, must be the province of Modern Poetry for some time to come—to give pleasure and to throw light upon the human heart.[22]

His attitude toward the accomplishments of contemporary poets was compounded of cheerful resignation and moderate optimism:

It is possibly true that, at the present time, we have among us no figure that is very monumental. . . . But if, at the present moment, we have no very great figure . . . in poetry we have no great figure anywhere.[23]

He considered the great defect of modern poetry to be its derivative character; it too frequently takes its impressions not from life, but from books. "Most of the verse that is written today deals in a derivative manner with medieval emotions."[24] But it is a defect easily remedied, and when the poet turns "inquiring, sincere, and properly humble eyes upon the life that is around him," when he once again speaks

[22] *Ibid.*, 183.
[23] *Ibid.*, 173.
[24] "Modern Poetry," *The Living Age*, Vol. XLVI, No. 3419 (January 15, 1910), 182.

in the language of his time, "such language as he ordinarily uses," then poetry will come into its own again.[25] In the work of Yeats, De la Mare, Flint, Lawrence, and Pound, Hueffer detected the basis for his hope: "gradually it has forced itself upon us that there is a new quality, a new power of impressionism that is open to poetry."[26]

When he had to explain his own verse technique, Hueffer was less certain. He could explain his method of prose composition glibly enough, but "with verse I just do not know: I do not know anything at all. As far as I am concerned, it just comes . . . the writing of verse hardly appears to me to be a matter of work: it is a process as far as I am concerned, too uncontrollable."[27] Nevertheless, he strove to attain very definite characteristics. He tried to avoid the "poetic" attitude, the artificial frame of mind which the attempt to write poetry seems to encourage, to avoid being "literary." His own poetic aim was simply "to register my own times in terms of my own time"; to use "the language of my own day, a language clear enough for certain matters, employing a slang where slang is felicitous and vulgarity where it seems to me that vulgarity is the only weapon against dullness."[28] Finally, he wanted to register easily and naturally the passing emotions which are the modern poet's material.

The one poem of Hueffer's which appeared under the Imagist label is exactly what one would expect from his theory. "In the Little Old Market Place" is a descriptive

[25] *The Critical Attitude*, 190.

[26] Preface, *Collected Poems* (London, 1914), 25.

[27] "Impressionism—Some Speculations—I," *Poetry*, Vol. II, No. 5 (August, 1913), 178; "The Poet's Eye," *The New Freewoman*, Vol. I, No. 6 (September 1, 1913), 107.

[28] Preface, *Collected Poems*, 28.

poem whose subject is the Grande Place of a small western European town. Seen by the poet on the late afternoon of a rainy day, the Place impressed him as dismal, dull, lonely, yet possessed of a certain charm. Without direct statement of his own feeling, he recreated his impression, selecting a series of visual images which had contributed most strongly to it. He uses few metaphors or similes, nor does he employ the symbol: only the scene itself and the immediate impression it creates are important. Consistent with his theory, he writes a verse form whose lines are of irregular length but achieve a kind of regularity through the recurrence of an anapestic foot and heavily accentuated rhymes. The result suggests the quaint, balladlike poem which he hoped to see in modern poetry. "On Heaven," which almost appeared in the anthology of 1915, has a similar metric and uses the same descriptive, pictorial method to create Hueffer's impression of Heaven, which he whimsically associates with the leisurely, sidewalk-café life of a small town in southern France.

Like Hulme, Hueffer considered it expedient to take a hitch in poetry's belt. He wanted the poet to be less ambitious, to treat the fleeting, personal moods which he unquestionably can know; to avoid the symbolism that tries to reach beyond the known to knowledge which must be vague and can be given only vague expression; to transform ordinary facts into phenomena seen imaginatively and to give poetry a quality of hardness by the intellectual effort required in this process; and, above all, to avoid the "literary," to speak in the natural, intelligible language of prose. However, although the similarities are many and striking, one should not carry them too far. Hueffer's Impressionism was similar to Hulme's Imagism in that it was fashioned to avoid the direct statement; but it differed in avoiding, at the same time, "words that stuck out of sentences either by their brilliant unusualness or their 'amazing aptness.' " Either sort of word, he felt, arrests the reader's attention and " 'hangs up' " both the meaning and cadence of a phrase. As an Impressionist, Hueffer wanted the reader "to forget the writer—to forget that he was reading. We wished him to be hypnotized into thinking that he was living what he read—or, at least, into the conviction that he was listening to a simple and in no way brilliant narrator who was telling—not writing—a true story."[29] He was here describing his prose technique, which perhaps accounts for some of the difference, but it would not account for all; in his poetry also he avoided the amazingly apt word or phrase. Hueffer's Impressionism might be described as Hulme's Imagism without the *éclat* of the clever analogy, though the distinction is one of degree, for, in either case, the artist renders by seeing the object imaginatively. And the similarities are forceful enough to give some substance to Hueffer's claims for his own relationship to the poetry of the anthologies.

[29] *Return to Yesterday* (New York, 1932), 216–17.

VI

Ezra Pound and Imagist Theory

AT ONE TIME or another during the five-year history of Imagism no fewer than thirteen poets, including Ezra Pound, H. D., James Joyce, William Carlos Williams, and D. H. Lawrence, acknowledged at least ostensible service to its doctrine. Its principles were declared not once but three times: in *Poetry* for March, 1913, and then in the prefaces to the 1915 and 1916 anthologies. Pound was largely responsible for the original manifesto, and it was he who guided the editing and publication of *Des Imagistes;* but supervision of the three succeeding anthologies passed into the hands of other poets, who wrote their own theory. If Imagism reflected such a variety of interests, perhaps it cannot be studied as the development of a single idea.

Certain factors, however, suggest that this approach may not be unprofitable. In spite of the frequent addition of new members, and the equally frequent disappearance of old, three poets (Aldington, Flint, and H. D.) continued their allegiance to the movement from 1912 to 1917, and two others (Pound and Amy Lowell) for periods almost as long. Further, the Imagists leaned heavily upon the leadership of Ezra Pound and Amy Lowell; strong enough to enforce their wishes, these two would have been disinclined either to accept poetry or to join in the publication of manifestoes which did not conform to their standards. Though Pound relinquished his leadership in favor of Amy Lowell, their differences were editorial rather than aesthetic and stemmed chiefly from the fact that the movement was not big enough to include both of them; they arranged a separation on aesthetic grounds because this seemed the more mannerly and tactful explanation to offer the public. Only as personal relations became more and more strained did the poets of the two factions begin to criticize one another for corrupting the original doctrine; and it is worth noting that under no circumstances did one accuse the other of having deserted Imagism for another poetic theory.

Doctrinaire Imagism must be studied through its manifestoes, but since they are by nature fairly general, they can best be clarified and illustrated by reference to the ideas of those who were primarily responsible for them. Therefore in this chapter the introduction and exposition of Imagist doctrine by Ezra Pound will be examined; his interpretation of the theory, the sources from which his understanding of it grew, and its influence upon his development as a poet will be considered. Pound is of sufficient importance to modern poetry that a part of Imagism's historical significance might derive from its relationship to his art.

I.

Pound's chief interest during the years before he became the leader of Imagism was the pre-Renaissance literature of southern Europe. After his arrival in London in 1908, he applied to the University of Pennsylvania for a continuation of the fellowship he had been granted in 1906. Three requests of this kind were denied, but he went on with his studies and soon began to acquire some scholarly reputation. In 1909, he gave a series of lectures sponsored by the Polytechnic, located on Regent Street in London. The prospectus announced lectures on "The Development of the Literature of Southern Europe" by Ezra Pound, M.A. The opening lecture was to be given free; five others rounded out the brief course; if these were successful, they were to be followed by a longer series later in the year. He also gave an occasional private lecture, one of which, delivered under the chairmanship of W. P. Ker, Aldington has described in *Life for Life's Sake*.

Pound incorporated some of the results of his medieval studies into books and articles, which began to appear in 1910. *The Spirit of Romance* was an "attempt to define the charm of the pre-Renaissance literature of Latin Europe." In it he candidly disclaimed any intention of producing a work of philology or comparative literature; his interest, he said, was in poetry. The next year he contracted to write for *The New Age* a series of articles "in illustration of 'The New Method' in scholarship." Called "I Gather the Limbs of Osiris," the articles offered discussions, and in some cases translations, of the poetry in which Pound was most steeped. Another article, on the troubadours, was accepted and published by *The Quarterly Review*. A translation of *The Sonnets and Ballate of Guido Cavalcanti*, which appeared in print in 1912, was his last major scholarly effort during this period.

As indicated by his comment in *The Spirit of Romance*, Pound was conducting his studies mainly with a view to sharpening his skill as a poet:

I think the artist should master all known forms and systems of metric, and I have with some persistence set about doing this, searching particularly into those periods wherein the systems came to birth or attained their maturity. It has been complained, with some justice, that I dump my notebooks on the public.[1]

Because he felt that it was the basis for all modern European poetry, he had concentrated upon the lyric tradition of Provence, and his early poetry shows clearly the influence of these studies. In the volumes published between 1908 and 1912, there are translations from Provençal, as well as Anglo-Saxon and German. There are attempts to reproduce in English the effect or spirit of an older poetry: "*Na Audiart*" is a troubadour song, and the Villonauds are "what I conceive after a good deal of study to be an expression akin to, if not of, the spirit breathed in Villon's own poetry."

Not all of his sources, however, were so remote in time or place. Poems like "The Tree" and "Night Litany" show his interest in Yeats and in a Swinburnian conception of poetic beauty; but this early work more often reflects an admiration for Browning, for his language and rhythms and especially for the genre he perfected.[2] Many of Pound's poems are what he referred to as "dramatic lyrics," which he described as

the poetic part of a drama the rest of which—to me the prose part—is left to the reader's immagination [sic] or implied or set

---

[1] "Prolegomena," *The Poetry Review*, Vol. II (February, 1912), 73.

[2] He acknowledged his debt to Browning in "Mesmerism" and in "Fifine," which he said was intended to answer "the question quoted from Browning's own 'Fifine at the Fair.'"

in a short note. I catch the character I happen to be interested in at the moment he interests me. Usualy [sic] a moment of song, self-analysis, or sudden understanding, . . . and the rest of the play would bore me and presumably the reader. I paint my man as I conceive him, et voila toute!

The dramatic lyrics frequently recreate a personality whom he has discovered in the course of his studies. The monologue of *"La Fraisne"* is spoken by a character taken from a Provençal story ("the man is whole or half mad"); "Sestina," whose metrical form is also borrowed from the troubadours, portrays the vigorous, war-loving Bertrans de Born.

Early in 1912, however, he began to express doubt about the poetry he was writing. The very fact that his first volumes had found some favor with the critics made him suspect that they lacked originality. In "Salutation the Second" he admitted feeling that he had reached an audience only because he was as far behind the times as the audience itself usually is. "Prolegomena," in February of 1912, offered an elaborate criticism and defense of his own work to that date.

No good poetry is ever written in a manner twenty years old, for to write in such a manner shows conclusively that the writer thinks from books, convention and *cliché*, and not from life, yet a man feeling the divorce of life and his art may naturally try to resurrect a forgotten mode if he find in that mode some leaven, or if he think he see in it some element lacking in contemporary art which may unite that art again to its sustenance, life.

Through his critical writing one can trace the desire to modernize his poetry and his way of talking about art. Unfortunately, he expressed his theories in a hastily written prose—he was anything but a systematic thinker; and, as he was primarily interested in poetry rather than aesthetics, theory was of less importance to him than it was to Hulme. Yet he assumed the functions of the critic and theorist, he obviously wrote his "Contemporania" of 1912 to suit certain standards he considered new for his time, and it is of some importance to know his version of what these standards were.

At first, his aesthetic was little more than opinion about what he did and did not like in poetry. A letter to W. C. Williams deserves quotation, not only as a sample of Pound's poetics at this period but as an interesting and entertaining illustration of Poundian whimsy.

Here are a list of facts on which U and 9,000,000 other poets have spieled endlessly.

1. Spring is a pleasant season.
   The flowers, etc. etc. sprout bloom etc., etc.
2. Young man's fancy   lightly
                        heavily
                        gaily etc. etc.
3. Love   , a delightsome tickling
                  indefinable, etc.
                  by day, etc. etc. etc.,
                  by night, etc. etc. etc.
4. Trees, bells, etc. are by a provident
   nature arranged diversely in diverse
   places.
5. Winds, clouds, rains, etc.
   flop through and over 'em.

6. Men love women
   (More poetic in singular but the
   verb retains the same form)

in the above 6 groups I think you find
the bulk of the ages—wait.

7. Men fight battles, etc.
8. Men go on voyages, etc.

The same letter contained an informal statement of Pound's positive views:

I don't know that I can make much of a list.

1. To paint the thing as I see it.
2. Beauty.
3. Freedom from didacticism.
4. It is only good manners if you repeat a few other men to at least do it better or more briefly.—utter originality is of course out of the question. Besides, the Punch Bowl covers that point.

Aside from his insistence upon an honest and precise rendering of subject matter and upon craftsmanship rather than "inspiration," there is one point especially worth noting: the inclination toward an art-for-art's-sake doctrine, emphasizing beauty and freedom from didacticism as two of the primary aims of art.

It was not long, however, before Pound began to state his theories more fully. His concept of art first developed in the direction implied by his letter to Williams; during the next two years he defended even more specifically his assertion that art need have no message, make no criticism

of life, that its justification is its beauty. In 1910, he defined
its purpose: "Great art is made, not to please, but to call
forth, or create, an ecstasy. The finer the quality of this
ecstasy, the finer the art."[3] The ecstasy of which he spoke
would have a spiritual rather than a physical basis: it would
be evoked only by "that subtler understanding which is
genius, and the dayspring of the arts." Coleridge and Dante
provided him with the definitions of beauty he found most
satisfactory, Coleridge's in terms of spirits calling to the
soul, Dante's in terms of melody that draws or attracts the
soul to it—both apparently consistent with the ideals of
the nineties ("a manner twenty years old") and at odds
with those defended by Hulme, though Pound does allow
that art may serve its function of relieving ennui not only
by creating sheer beauty, ecstasy, "splendour of thought,"
but by some "lightning turn of phrase."

In less than a year his discussions of art begin to assume
a more practical tone. He insists that the artist admit responsibilities similar to those of the psychologist; he in-
structs him to seek out the facts or " 'luminous details' which
govern knowledge as a switchboard does a circuit," so that
his work will remain "the permanent basis of psychology
and metaphysics";[4] and by 1913, the trend toward a more
practical, more modern terminology has become unmis-
takable. He describes the arts as a science whose subject
is man:

The arts, literature, poesy, are a science, just as chemistry is a
science. Their subject is man, mankind and the individual. . . .

[3] *The Spirit of Romance* (London, 1910), 81.
[4] "I Gather . . . ," *The New Age*, Vol X, No. 8 (December 21, 1911),
178; *ibid.*, Vol. X, No. 6 (December 7, 1911), 130.

The arts give us a great percentage of the lasting and unassailable data regarding the nature of man, of immaterial man, of man considered as a thinking and sentient creature. . . . No science save the arts will give us the requisite data for learning in what ways men differ.[5]

Appropriately, the standard for good art is now expressed more frequently in terms of precision than in terms of beauty. "The touchstone of an art is its precision. . . . Bad art is inaccurate art. It is art that makes false reports. . . . By good art. . . . I mean the art that is most precise." There is no sharp break, however, for Pound had by no means ignored the importance of precision—*The Spirit of Romance* praises Dante's precision in revealing exactly the thing he had seen; Daniel and Cavalcanti showed him a precision he could not find in the Victorians. The ecstasy cannot, in fact, be conveyed without preciseness of formal definition. The difference is merely a matter of emphasis: the word *beauty* grows much less ubiquitous, as if Pound were beginning to consider it outmoded.

When in 1914, he wrote: "The organization of forms is a much more energetic and creative action than the copying or imitating of light on a haystack,"[6] and appeared as the advocate of abstract as opposed to representational art, he made this emphasis more apparent. He condemned natural beauty as a false criterion, though, of course, he did not mean that nature is not the source of beauty—only that the artist must depend not on nature's beauty but on his

[5] "The Serious Artist," *The New Freewoman*, Vol. I, No. 9 (October 15, 1913), 161, 163.

[6] "Vorticism," *The Fortnightly Review*, Vol. XCVI, No. dlxxiii (September 1, 1914), 470.

own handling and ordering of the forms nature offers him, on his own expressive techniques developed from the medium in which he is working.

Similar changes occurred between 1908 and 1917 in his discussions of the poet's art. His early comments recommend that the poet avoid being too explicit, but again it is necessary to add that his description of poetry as an equation for the emotions dates from 1910. "The poet must never infringe upon the painter's function; the picture must exist around the words; the words must not attempt too far to play at being brush strokes."[7] He allows the claim for exactness, but is in 1912 still writing of poetry as an art that conveys the "indefinite, impalpable" things of life.[8] A year later he is speaking of poetry as a "communication between intelligent men," whose aim should be " 'maximum efficiency of expression.' "[9] He demands that its language approximate the language of intelligent conversation. He sets for it the same measure of accomplishment he expects of prose and is willing to condemn any poem whose communicative value does not compare favorably with that of prose statement. The distinction that he makes between the two is that poetry is more "highly energized" and its language more dignified.

Before 1912, he showed no specialized interest in image or metaphor. He alluded to the function of metaphor in Dante's poetry and pointed out Dante's skill in expressing relationships suddenly and swiftly perceived. Moreover,

[7] *The Spirit of Romance,* 65.

[8] "I Gather . . . ," *The New Age,* Vol. X, No. 13 (January 25, 1912), 301.

[9] "The Serious Artist," *The New Freewoman,* Vol. I, No. 9 (October 15, 1913), 213.

he praised both Dante and Daniel for the vividness of their similes, a vividness achieved by use of particular, concrete phenomena, giving the natural picture. Pound's *beauty* in these years was, in fact, associated with a particular kind of imagery which he called "pure poetry." The passages he praises most highly often contain imagery of light (the description of Durendal in the *Chanson de Roland* as gleaming, flaming white in the sun) or imagery that catches a delicate natural motion (the simile in which Dante compares himself to the spray which bows its tip in the wind); and this imagery, as Pound notes, reflects accurate observation of things in nature or the natural process.

"Prolegomena" in February, 1912, spoke of the symbol rather than the image or metaphor but concentrated again upon the natural.

I believe that the proper and perfect symbol is the natural object, that if a man use "symbols" he must so use them that their symbolic function does not obtrude; so that *a* sense, and the poetic quality of the passage, is not lost to those who do not understand the symbol as such, to whom, for instance, a hawk is a hawk.

Although the warning against a private symbolism is appropriate to his standard of precision, and although he would undoubtedly have been sympathetic toward Hulme's attack upon vagueness and imprecision, he gives no hint that he advocated or even knew of Hulme's imagism. While the *Poetry* manifesto in 1913 spoke of the Image, it also repeated Pound's earlier assertion that the natural object is always the adequate symbol; but before the close of the year, he elaborated upon the *Poetry* definition, related the Image, or image, to the metaphor, and, as he had done in

1910, referred the reader to Aristotle's *Poetics* for a discussion of metaphor in poetry.

Aristotle will tell you that "the apt use of metaphor being as it is, the swift perception of relations, is the true hall-mark of genius." That abundance, that readiness of the image is indeed one of the surest proofs that the mind is upborne upon the emotional surge.[10]

When one looks again at the parenthesis defining *apt use* as *swiftness,* he sees a striking resemblance between Pound's understanding of the function of metaphor and Hulme's, especially when he realizes the rather suddenly increased attention Pound is giving to this element in poetry.

As early as 1910 he stated a belief that poetry stands in closer relation to music, painting, and sculpture than to any part of literature which is not pure poetry; but in 1914 he restated this with a somewhat different emphasis. Before, he had been trying to minimize the significance of poetry as philosophy; now he is more concerned with enlarging upon the melodic, visual, plastic impact of its language, and classifying poetry on the basis of the kind of "non-literary" appeal that it makes. His awareness of image and metaphor as expressive devices is more definite, his insistence upon their importance more explicit.

There have always been two sorts of poetry which are, for me at least, the most "poetic"; they are firstly, the sort of poetry which seems to be music just forcing itself into articulate speech, and, secondly, that sort of poetry which seems as if sculpture or painting were just forced or forcing itself into words. The gulf be-

10 *Ibid.,* 195.

131

tween evocation and description, in this latter case, is the un-
bridgeable difference between genius and talent.[11]

Pound proceded to justify Imagism as natural and inevitable in poetry. By 1915 he was arguing that energy, or
emotion, the material of all art, will at times present itself
to the mind in the form of an image. When it does so, it
must become poetry rather than some other art like painting,
which is appropriate when emotion produces "patterns" in
the mind. The image (or Image) may be subjective, shaped
by the mind into something which does not resemble the
external object responsible for its existence; or it may be
objective, clearly recognizable as an external object but
stripped by the mind of all but its dominant or dramatic
qualities. While Pound does not offer examples of either
type, one might venture the diving scene in Mallarmé's
"*Petit Air*" as illustrating the subjective and the last two
lines of Eliot's "Preludes" the objective.

> *The worlds revolve like ancient women*
> *Gathering fuel in vacant lots.*[12]

"In either case the Image is more than an Idea. It is a vortex
or cluster of fused ideas and is endowed with energy."[13]
And in either case, Pound has evolved a theory which by
1914 and 1915 he is expounding with characteristic single-
mindedness. He praises the Image for its directness ("The
image is itself the speech . . . the word beyond formulated

[11] "The Later Yeats," *Poetry*, Vol. IV, No. 11 (May, 1914), 68.

[12] "Preludes," *Collected Poems*, 1909–35 (New York, 1936), 68.

[13] "Affirmations," *The New Age, Vol.* XVI, No. 13 (January 28,
1915), 349.

language,"[14] echoing a statement made in 1910); for its ability to free poetry from rhetoric; and he even refers to Dante's *Paradiso* as an Image, extending the term to mean not the single device but the total structure, the impression made by the poem as a whole.

Only in regard to metrics does he maintain a position whose statement does not vary appreciably from 1908 to 1917, though even here he can be seen adopting modern terminology. The recurrent theme of his discussions of metric is the close relation between poetry and music; and, in spite of his interest in Imagism, it was this preoccupation with which he began and to which he returned after he gave up advertising his "school."

He based his argument upon the importance of rhythm to both arts. "Rhythm is perhaps the most primal of all things known to us. It is basic in poetry and music mutually."[15] Rhythm, he said, is basic in music because it determines pitch and melody; pitch depends upon the frequency with which sound vibrations strike the ear; by varying frequency, one varies pitch, and these variations in pitch produce melody. For the same reasons, rhythm is basic in poetry: the pitch of a vowel or consonant sound depends upon the frequency of its vibrations; by varying frequency, one gets either a higher or lower sound, and the variation of these sounds produces the melody of a poetic line. Pound's theory emphasizes mainly the pitch of words and considers rhythm from the point of view of duration, or quantity (synonymous, in at least one article, with fre-

[14] "Vorticism," *The Fortnightly Review*, Vol. XCVI, No. dlxxiii (September 1, 1914), 466.

[15] *The Sonnets and Ballate of Guido Cavalcanti* (Boston, 1912), xxii.

quency), rather than stress, though he does consider stress as a part of the music of poetry.

The rhythm is a matter of duration of individual sounds and of stress, and the matter of the "word melody" depends largely on the fitness of this duration and stress to the sounds wherewith it is connected.[16]

Extending his analogy, he argued that each emotion has an absolute rhythmical pattern which alone gives it adequate expression. As emotion organizes visible forms, so it organizes audible forms, and if the poet is capable of fully comprehending his emotion, he will express it in a rhythm which exactly corresponds to it and will thus be able to re-create the exact emotion in others. "When this rhythm, or when the vowel and consonantal melody or sequence seems truly to bear the trace of emotion which the poem . . . is intended to communicate, we say that this part of the work is good."[17] Further, as in music it should be possible to determine the complete form of a composition from the pattern of overtones, so in poetry "the rhythm set in a line . . . connotes its symphony, which, had we a little more skill, we could score for an orchestra."[18]

While his theory leads toward a quantitative rather than an accentual verse, it also leads to a "free" verse form; by 1914 Pound was so influential a champion of *vers libre* that, according to Eliot, *vers libristes* who wished to see their work in print had first to submit their work for Pound's

[16] "The Approach to Paris," *The New Age*, Vol. XIII, No. 25 (October 16, 1913), 350.
[17] "The Serious Artist," *The New Freewoman*, Vol. 1, No. 9 (October 15, 1913), 194.
[18] *The Sonnets and Ballate, xxii.*

approval.[19] He reasoned that if each emotion has an appropriate rhythm, then the poet can be bound by no conventional rules, and metrical patterns will be as varied as the emotions themselves. On this ground, he even repudiated the French recommendation that *vers libre* must be given a certain regularity by the repetition of a "constant." "A man's rhythm must be interpretative, it will be, therefore, in the end, his own, uncounterfeiting, uncounterfeitable."[20] In defense of free verse, he cited authority in the classics, pointing, for example, to several passages from the plays of Euripides, and he drew another analogy with music: because the musician composes in four-four time, he is not required to use four quarter notes to each bar. "To apply this musical truism to verse is to employ *vers libre*";[21] *vers libre* was not, for Pound, associated with complete freedom but with variations within a given norm, the unit or block of time.

It was not long before Pound realized the possible implications of his argument. "The discovery that bad *vers libre* can be quite as bad as any other sort of bad verse is by no means modern."[22] The difficulty was inevitable; poets assumed that free verse meant complete freedom from form. By the time he had made the discovery for his own generation, it was too late to do more than offer a few recommendations and set a corrective example. He referred poets to Arnold Dolmetsch's book on the interpretation of music which advised by quotation that the composer "break time" only after he has mastered the fundamentals of music

[19] See Taupin, *L'Influence* . . . , 115.

[20] "Prolegomena," *The Poetry Review,* Vol. II (February, 1912), 73.

[21] "The Tradition," *Poetry,* Vol. III, No. 4 (January, 1914), 140.

[22] "Affirmations," *The New Age,* Vol. XVI, No. 13 (January 28, 1915), 350.

and that he understand time as quantity and equality of beats, cadence as a "soul" that must be added to them. A note to *Pavannes and Divisions* (1917):

I think one should write *vers libre* only when one "must" . . . when the "thing" builds up a rhythm more beautiful than that of set metres, or more real, more a part of the emotion of the "thing," more germane, intimate, interpretative than the measure of regular accentual verse; . . . Eliot has said the thing very well when he said, "No *vers* is *libre* for the man who wants to do a good job."[23]

At the same time Pound reasserted his opinion that progress would not come from *vers libre* but from an attempt to approximate classical quantitative metres, and he published objections to another statement by Eliot which implied that metres are measured by accent. To Harriet Monroe he wrote in January of 1908:

I shall probably do some more work on sound. Anything really made to speak or sing is bound to lose on the page, unless the reader have some sense of sound . . . the *vers libre* public are probably by now as stone blind to the vocal or oral properties of a poem as the "sonnet" public was seven years ago to the actual language, i.e., all that has made my stuff interesting since Contemporania.

Pound's comments on art and poetry during these years reveal, then, less a change of direction than a change of emphasis and vocabulary. He has less to say of beauty and the soul and more of efficiency and precision; he rather sud-

[23] *Pavannes and Divisions* (New York, 1918), 108.

denly becomes eloquent on the importance of the image, or, as he sometimes called it, the Image, and metaphor in poetry; he relates his theories of metric to current theories of *vers libre*. Yet the Imagist, potentially present in the letter to Williams, can be seen all through the studies of the romance poets. He had gone to the past because he could there better observe creative vigor and mastery of technical problems, but he was becoming aware that he would have to develop his own mode of expression, conditioned by and adapted to the consciousness of his own age. And his tentative suggestions regarding a poetry appropriate to his time took this form in 1912:

it will, I think, move against poppycock, it will be harder and saner, it will be what Mr. Hewlett calls, "nearer the bone." It will be as much like granite as it can be, its force will be in its truth, its interpretative power (of course, poetic force does always rest there); . . . We will have fewer painted adjectives impeding the shock and stroke of it. At least for myself, I want it so, austere, direct, free from emotional slither.

In this year he set about to bring his own poems up to date, partly by applying these standards to them, standards that he had seen in the literature of the past. Late in 1912, he forwarded to Harriet Monroe a series of poems, published under the title of "Contemporania," which was the first result of his efforts at modernizing his own work and providing a model for others. An accompanying letter said he hoped that these poems would break through conventional surfaces, the surfaces of the nineties that still characterized his verse and that of his contemporaries, and would be of use in building the new art of language and metre.

Although the "Prolegomena" had stated explicitly that when he called for a new poetry he was not thinking in terms of a crusading movement which would rally other poets around the principles of modernism or any other -ism, he confided later to Alice Henderson that his "*Contemporania*" series was a "sort of preparation for the oncoming horror. It's not futurism, and it's not post-impressionism but it's work contemporary with these schools." Perhaps he was beginning to wonder whether a program for the new poetry might not profit by being presented as a militant aesthetic movement similar to those which were attracting attention at the time. In the summer of 1912, he had first referred to a poem as "Imagiste," and in November he published his *Ripostes* with the appendix containing Hulme's poems and the prefatory note which introduced *Les Imagistes* as descendants of Hulme's 1909 club. In the spring of 1913, he presented the first Imagist manifesto. The Imagist movement, then, followed closely upon Pound's realization that his own poetic method was out of date.

2.

Pound once stated that a poet who wished to discuss his art had to supplement Hulme's Frith Street evenings, which were given to metaphysical speculation, with afternoons at South Lodge. Late in 1912, he wrote: "I would rather talk about poetry with Ford Madox Hueffer than with any man in London";[24] and by 1914, his admiration had so increased that he could declare Hueffer to be the best critic in England. More recently, he has thought it necessary to reaffirm

[24] "Status Rerum," *Poetry*, Vol. I, No. 4 (January, 1913), 124.

these judgments and to point out that Hueffer was the "CRITICAL LIGHT of the 1912 period."[25]

At least one of Hueffer's strictures was certainly applicable to Pound. He persistently criticized the modern poet for dealing with books rather than life and with medieval rather than modern emotions. Though he mentioned no names in his published articles, the criticism obviously bore special relevance to his close friend, Pound, then deeply buried in study of the troubadours, writing poetry which was unashamedly derivative. More than once discussion at South Lodge must have centered upon this very point.

But Hueffer was also ready to provide a new formula to replace the old one which he had encouraged the poet to abandon. He recommended that the writer deal with his "own times" by rendering personal impressions of them; urged him to consider his art as a science of human nature, entitled to the same respect due the other sciences which so completely usurp the admiration of modern man; and he insisted that the poet express his material in terms of his own time, in the nonliterary language of conversation, or, in other words, that poetic be at least as efficient as prose communication.

Hueffer's importance to Pound is much like that of the modern French poets: at a time when he was seeking ways of bringing new life to contemporary poetry, Hueffer through his criticism formulated an attitude and a series of standards that were applicable to the problem of literature as Pound saw it. His respect for Hueffer was based upon a belief that he was making important "experiments in modernity"; he described him as "searching—perhaps a little

[25] "This Hulme Business," *The Townsman*, Vol. II, No. 5 (January, 1939), 15.

nonchalantly, but no matter—for a vital something which has in too great a degree slipped out of modern poetry."[26] A year later he began to quote Hueffer, on different occasions praising both Fletcher and the French poet Laurent Tailhade for rendering their own times. Thus it does not seem unreasonable to suggest that when Pound suddenly began talking about art (and poetry) as a science revealing data concerning "immaterial man," about the artist as psychologist, about a poetry whose language would equal the precision and communicative value of the best prose, he was echoing the language of Hueffer's criticism.

He maintained certain reservations about Hueffer's ideas. He felt, for example, that the language of Hueffer's poetry inclined too far toward the conversational and missed the dignity and intensity, the dynamic quality, which should characterize the diction of poetry. But he expressed a more fundamental dissatisfaction with the Impressionistic technique:

Impressionism belongs to paint, it is of the eye. . . . Poetry is in some odd way concerned with the specific gravity of things, with their nature . . . their nature *and* show, if you like; with the relation between them, but not with the show alone.

The *conception* of poetry is a process more intense than the *reception* of an impression. And no impression, however carefully articulated, can, recorded, convey that feeling of sudden light which the works of art should and must convey.[27]

In so stating his criticism, he effectively summarized the dif-

[26] "The Book of the Month," *The Poetry Review*, Vol. I, No. 3 (March, 1912), 134.
[27] *Ibid.*, 133.

ference between Impressionism and Hulme's imagism: the Impressionist records, the Imagist reveals by showing new relations; the Impressionist gives you his view of certain phenomena, and his view should be original or its expression cannot be justified; but he does not communicate the "feeling of sudden light," evoked by skillful handling of analogy, which requires that the artist penetrate to the essential meaning of his material.

The Image became central in Pound's theory at the time when he began to speak as the founder of the Imagist movement. The manifesto which he published in 1913, however, enveloped this aspect of the new doctrine in an atmosphere of mystery.

1. Direct treatment of the "thing," whether subjective or objective.

2. To use absolutely no word that did not contribute to the presentation.

3. As regarding rhythm: to compose in sequence of the musical phrase, not in sequence of a metronome.

They held also a certain "Doctrine of the Image," which they had not committed to writing; they said that it did not concern the public, and would provoke useless discussion.

In the companion article, to which Pound signed his name, there was interesting elaboration upon this last statement:

An "Image" is that which presents an intellectual and emotional complex in an instant of time. I use the term "complex" rather in the technical sense employed by the newer psychologists, such as Hart, though we might not agree absolutely in our application.

It is the presentation of such a "complex" instantaneously which gives that sense of sudden liberation; that sense of freedom from time limits and space limits; that sense of sudden growth, which we experience in the presence of the greatest works of art.

It is better to present one Image in a lifetime than to produce voluminous works.

The definition seems specific and it is often quoted; but it is also elastic enough to allow such a variety of illustration and example that it could not have helped define the practice of a school, especially as Pound did not trouble here to show the way in which the Imagists interpreted it.

There is little in the first three principles that Pound had not said, in one way or another, before 1913. He had condemned verbiage in poetry, concentrating with special vigor upon the superfluous adjective. His letter to Williams in October, 1908, had specified that, since originality is out of the question, one had best, when repeating what has already been said, use as few words as possible. Two years later he had tried to clarify the proper and functional uses of the adjective. He recognized epithets of primary apparition (those which describe what is actually presented to the sense of vision), secondary apparition (those which are an afterthought, like "forbidden tree"), and emotional apparition (those which are meant, impressionistically, to evoke a feeling, like "bitter *black* wind"). Finally, as has already been said his "Prolegomena," in 1912, declared that the new poetry would have "fewer painted adjectives impeding the shock and stroke of it."

Moreover, the statement on the rhythm of verse was Pound's own, for he persistently argued with those who tried to force emotional expression into preconceived metrical patterns. Every emotion, on the contrary, has its appropriate rhythm, and rhythms will consequently be as varied as the shades of emotion which they express. Nor can one assert that he had not before advocated "direct treatment"; directness was, implicitly, a virtue he sought and found in the romance writers he had studied. Nevertheless, he so explained the principle that it was clearly dependent upon the doctrine of the Image: it means that "having got the Image, one refrains from hanging it with festoons."[28] And, while he had by no means ignored the communicative powers of image, metaphor, and the language "beyond metaphor," he had, again, not explicitly given to this aspect of poetry the central position it now had—at least if the title of the new school and the hints offered in its manifestoes were to be followed to their suggested conclusions.

Flint, whose name was affixed to "Imagisme," had no doubt concerning the source of Pound's theories about the Image. As previously pointed out, his "History" accused him of having borrowed it from T. E. Hulme; and a letter to Amy Lowell, giving the background for the article, stated the case even more succinctly, brushing aside any question of credit to Pound for originating Imagist doctrine and asserting that he (and presumably others) had taken the remarks appended to *Ripostes* as a joke at Hulme's expense, not as a serious effort to found a *new* school of poetry. Actually, said Flint, Pound's contribution was only his mastery of the advertiser's technique. Two remarks by

[28] "Affirmations," *The New Age*, Vol. XVI, No. 13 (January 28, 1915), 350.

Fletcher support Flint's charge by proving that Pound knew Hulme's ideas well enough to have introduced them into his own doctrine. Describing a dinner to which the Imagists were invited by Amy Lowell, he says that Pound discoursed on H. D.'s Imagism, all the French theories of *vers libre* imaginable, and on Hulme's theories of language. Pound himself records a conversation with Hulme during which he brought to Hulme's attention the functional use of metaphor in Provençal poetry. Fletcher also attributes the polite hostility which characterized Hulme's attitude towards Pound after 1913 to Hulme's belief that the American was exploiting his ideas, and, more specifically, to the fact that *Ripostes* had included Hulme's poems without his permission. "Hulme was thoroughly angry."[29]

Pound's few remarks on his debt to Hulme are ambiguous but provide some basis for the statements by Flint and Fletcher. In *The Townsman*, he wrote: "I attempted to do Hulme justice in the last pages of *Ripostes*"; the "social document" at the close of *Des Imagistes* and the summary of a conversation with Hulme, which he included in the *Catholic Anthology*, hint that he either felt a continuing obligation to Hulme or saw some other reason for maintaining the association. Yet he refused to state the exact nature and extent of his debt; he cited Aristotle as his authority for the place of metaphor or analogy in poetry; and in *The New Age* took to himself the credit for contemporary "fo-

---

[29] This remark was made by Fletcher in a letter to the present writer. The others cited here are from *Life Is My Song* (New York, 1937), 88, 76. Jacob Epstein's comment on the Hulme-Pound relationship is interesting. "Someone once asked Hulme how long he would tolerate Ezra Pound, and Hulme thought for a moment, then said that he knew already exactly when he would have to kick him downstairs."—*Let There Be Sculpture* (New York, 1940), 54.

cus" on the Image. Since it is evident that he did have some knowledge of Hulme's theories, one can define his debt specifically only by comparison of Imagist doctrine as the two men understood it.

Imagism was in Pound's mind most closely associated with the poetry of H. D. The meetings in Kensington tea shops during the spring of 1912 had given him his first opportunity to study her work, and he immediately recognized her few poems as the kind of modern verse for which he had recently begun an intensive search. When he sent them to Harriet Monroe, late in 1912, his accompanying letter said:

am sending you some *modern* stuff by an American, I say modern, for it is in the laconic speech of the Imagistes, even if the subject is classic. . . . This is the sort of American stuff that I can show here and in Paris without its being ridiculed. Objective —no slither; direct—no excessive use of adjectives, no metaphors that won't permit examination. It's straight talk, straight as the Greek![30]

Plainly, the specific merits which he observed in her poetry foreshadowed the principles of the manifesto published early the next year. In fact, Pound has said that Imagism "was started, not very seriously, chiefly to give H. D.'s five poems a hearing";[31] and as late as the summer of 1914, he quoted her "Oread" as most fully illustrating its doctrine.

H. D.'s verse was certainly not written by any formula but her own. In it there is little of modern life, and on first glance it would not at all seem to satisfy Pound's recently

[30] Quoted by Harriet Monroe, *A Poet's Life*, 264.
[31] *Ibid.*, 267.

revised standards. It is intensely personal, rigidly limited by an attitude toward the world which she has analyzed in a few brief statements. She wrote to Williams in 1908:

I am, as you perhaps realize, more in sympathy with the odd and lonely—with those people that feel themselves apart from the whole—that are somewhat lost and torn and inclined to become embittered by that very loneliness.

As her interests at this time were apart from the main streams of life, so her poetry was written with little reference to it. When Amy Lowell asked for a brief autobiographical sketch, she replied: "my poems are so essentially reactions *from* life and things of pure imagination that I don't think details of my education, etc., would be valuable."

Though her isolation even prevented her from reading most contemporary poetry, she took her art seriously and tried to maintain very definite standards, particularly in regard to economical use of language. As *pro tempore* literary editor of *The Egoist*, she exercised her authority on one occasion by ruthlessly lopping off portions of a Williams poem which she felt were flippant, saying, "It's very well to mock at yourself—it is a spiritual sin to mock at your inspiration." In her own work, she pruned away all that might in any way be criticized as superfluous. A line from "The Pool" originally read, "I touch you with my thumb," but she eliminated the prepositional phrase before publication because it added nothing but assonance; and the typescript of "Storm" shows the following revisions in the interests of economy (the unitalicized words were marked out):

146

The branch is white
the green is *crushed,* and wet,
It is hurled out, of the trees,

Nor did she hesitate to brave Amy Lowell's authority when she felt it necessary to maintain her artistic integrity; she spoke against including Miss Lowell's "Turnpike" in an Imagist anthology because she found it inconsistent with Imagist doctrine.

The principal material of her early poems is an intensely concentrated reaction to some natural object, a reaction that is always evoked by the object as a physical thing. In "The Garden" she portrays the rose in terms of its hardness, not of its "prettiness," its beauty, or its symbolic significance. She feels its color as a physical quality and even gives a tangibility to the intense heat of a summer day. As Hulme recommended, she is here employing metaphor to assure that the reader reacts to a physical thing rather than a fuzzy and, at best, intangible abstraction. But her metaphor is felicitous by congruity rather than incongruity, the characteristic of the Hulme image; it sharpens meaning by apt comparison rather than striking analogy.

However, she did on occasion employ analogy for a purpose similar to that defined by Hulme. "Oread," which Pound consistently held up as a perfect illustration of Imagism, is based upon juxtaposition of ideas which on several counts more closely approximates the Hulme concept of poetry.

Whirl up, sea—
Whirl your pointed pines,
Splash your great pines

On our rocks,
Hurl your green over us,
Cover us with your pools of fir.

Metaphor here conveys not just a single sensation but a whole "complex" of impressions, to use the term employed by Pound in his manifesto, and this complex is the poem, for the poem is built upon a single metaphor. The comparison of the waves to fir trees gives not only pictorial outline, but color, a suggestion of coolness, softness, hushed sound, and even, perhaps, of fragrance. The personal feeling, the clarity, the hardness of the poem satisfy Hulme's requirements. Still, in spite of the directness achieved by the analogy, it does not emphasize the incongruity between the objects treated, nor does it attempt to translate the lofty and "poetic" sea into terms of the everyday and trivial.

If her poetry is not quite Hulme, it does, however, show the qualities Pound had praised in his troubadours—concreteness, accuracy of observation, swiftness of comparison, and beauty of image. Here was modern poetry which had the technical skill and the vitality he had thought he could not find in his contemporaries, adequate reason to found a school which might give this verse the publicity it deserved. Having observed the benefits derived from programs and manifestoes, Pound might well have taken some such method of getting H. D. into publication, regardless of Hulme, and the principles of the new school, such as they were, could conceivably have been much the same without his theory.

In defining Imagism from his own poetry, Pound selected

The apparition of these faces in the crowd;
Petals on a wet, black bough.[32]

The poem was written as an "equation" for a feeling evoked by the sudden glimpse of a few beautiful faces standing out of the crowd waiting to board a Paris subway train, and out of the dark, damp background of the station itself. As H. D.'s "Oread," it employs analogy to convey an "emotional complex"; the image of the petals is, as Pound said elsewhere, "itself the speech . . . the word beyond formulated language." It evokes impressions of delicate color; of texture, on the one hand soft and fragile and on the other rough, hard, and damp; it recreates the sharp contrast that demanded artistic expression.

Again, the poem is a single metaphor or simile, a clear indication that the Imagist sought to achieve his poetic effect through the single, dominant figure. Both terms of the metaphor were images of phenomena, images bringing language close to the hard, physical object. The second term of the comparison was chosen for the variety of sensuous connotations which it could bring to bear upon the first, especially striking impressions of color, light, and shadow. If, as the illustrations implied, this single metaphor was intended to carry the poem, then an Imagist poem was necessarily brief—a point further underlined by the sensuous character of the associations evoked. However, Imagist practice did not wholly substantiate this, and the fact is that Pound's examples were to a certain extent misleading; he seemed to be explaining the *i*mage when actually he was explaining the *I*mage—the total pattern, the organism or complex the poet succeeds in creating, a definition which

[32] "In a Station of the Metro," *Personae*, 104.

could theoretically apply to a poem of any length—though the two meanings were in his mind closely related. Finally, Pound's Imagism, like Hulme's was an apparent restriction of the limits of poetry, confining it to the limits of sensation and to the pleasure stimulated by realization of the artist's insight and sensitivity in perceiving fresh resemblances. For Pound, as well as Hulme, Imagism was a recognition that poetry must withdraw from ground on which it cannot compete with the scientist, but that within his own area, the area of human feeling which scientific language cannot express, the poet must emulate the scientist in the precision and efficiency of his language.

Around 1912–13 Pound had begun to concentrate upon this poetry of a brilliant, pictorial imagery he had seldom achieved or attempted before this time. "Fish and the Shadow" and "Phanopoeia," though belonging to a 1915 volume, are good examples. "Fish and the Shadow" opens with four imagistic statements about an object, the images suggesting first light, effortless motion, then the color of light, then the two combined. The meanings are handled so skillfully that the reader is just aware of the ambiguity which follows, when the shadow is spoken of in terms of its lightness. These connotations of light and even the vaguely disturbing ambiguity serve as effective introduction for the woman who at this point enters the poem.

Metaphor or swiftly revealed comparison, of course, is a part of this poem, but the nature of the insight produced lacks the fundamental irony of the Hulme technique. The complex which this and the other poems convey is, in fact, less dominated by the effect peculiar to striking analogy than by the beauty of the imagery of light, color, and texture —what Pound had in 1910 praised in passages from the romance writers as "pure poetry." His version of a modern, Imagistic verse reflected his own taste for beauty, and was little concerned with relating expressive techniques to a particular world view as Hulme had done. In spite of the changed tone of his critical pronouncements, *beauty* (of color, imagery of light and brightness) was still his aim; and even the apt or suddenly perceived metaphorical relation was perhaps less important in his Imagism than the clean, hard, beautiful visual image. Imagism was, as he had said, sculpture or painting just forcing itself into words— making the poem tend to brevity except in the most talented hands, but not necessarily brief; it was poetry which produced an Image, and the Image usually was dependent as much upon imagery of vivid natural detail as upon metaphor or analogy.

He called Yeats an Imagist on the strength of these lines from "The Magi":

Now as at all times I can see in the mind's eye,
In their stiff, painted clothes, the pale, unsatisfied ones
Appear and disappear in the blue depth of the sky
With all their ancient faces like rain-beaten stones
And all their helms of silver hovering side by side.[33]

And his own "Phanopoeia" (or "Imagism") shows clearly not only what, for him, constituted an Imagist poem, but what he had always admired, the kind of sharp, sheer beauty of image (and thus of Image) that is one of his principal achievements. The lines quoted are from the poem numbered *III* in the series.

[33] *Responsibilities* (New York, 1916).

AOI!
The whirling tissue of light
is woven and grows solid beneath us;
The sea-clear sapphire of air, the sea-dark clarity,
stretches both sea-cliff and ocean.

If these lines are Imagism, then his Imagism, in spite of what his best-known illustrations implied, was something more than just a poetry of objects or of objects illuminated by the yoking process of the metaphor. Here there is a greater effort to make the word fuse with the thing, the thing penetrating the shell of language and giving it a clarity of definition and sharpness of existence, a force of actuality which makes possible expression of intense feeling without the "slither" that accompanies the word in conventional (nonpoetic) usage. The word (or the poem) thus achieves its fullest apprehensible meaning—which suggests perhaps a limitation of the quality, if not the quantity, of meaning it can convey—a quality derived both from the kind of object it is and from the complex established by association of the qualities of this object with the qualities of others. But the process of definition and fusing is itself productive of force or energy. As he says elsewhere, "The god is inside the stone. . . . The force is arrested, but there is never any question about its latency, about the force being the essential." The importance of definition, in this literal sense, to Pound's work extends beyond definition of a beauty and has its complete elaboration only in *The Cantos*.

A desire to restore to language its ability to communicate "force" is the reason for Hulme's defense of metaphor, but its communication is not, as Pound shows, necessarily confined to metaphor and certainly not to the particular kind of metaphor that Hulme recommended. When Imagism gets into Pound's hands, it shares in the contemporary will to redefine poetry within a narrower area of operation, and yet at the same time gives this area a depth that was hardly suggested by what Imagism was, with some justice, taken to represent. It is not difficult to see, however, why Pound has been charged with indebtedness to Hulme. His attendance at Hulme's evenings, then his sudden attention to the Image must have seemed more than coincidental, especially since his note in *Ripostes* clearly suggested Imagism's descent from Hulme. And there are elements in Pound's writing that might be described as echoes of Hulme's doctrine, especially certain statements which could confirm Fletcher's report that he was interested in Hulme's theories of language. He predicted that the new poetry would be hard, would gain its effect through the force of its shock; and he spoke of the poet as "new-minting" language, which is constantly wearing out, and poetry as the language of exploration. Moreover, he insisted that Imagism differed from Symbolism for reasons which are precisely the ones Hulme would have given: "Imagisme is not symbolism. The symbolists dealt in 'association,' that is, in a sort of allusion, almost of allegory. They degraded the symbol to the status of a word . . . symbolism has usually been associated with mushy technique."[34] In his "Don'ts" he warned the poet specifically, though cautiously, against the Symbolist practice of defining one sense in terms of another, because such a practice may too easily become simply a substitute for finding the exact word. But all these remarks are characteristic of Pound, and the discussion returns again to

[34] "Vorticism," *The Fortnightly Review*, Vol. XCVI, No. dlxxiii (September 1, 1914), 463.

the fact that Imagism, for him, was, more than anything else, a concept of poetry which he evolved from his own principles of good writing.

The danger of too much emphasis upon Hulme may be shown in another way. Every one of the points made in paralleling Pound's Imagism with Hulme's might be made with equal validity in a comparison with Hueffer's theory; exception might be taken to the concentration upon the Image, but this did not mean to him exactly what Hulme had in mind, and even here Hueffer's "impression" provides a possible parallel. The difference between the impression and the image or Image, which Pound noted, perhaps accounts for his borrowing the name of his school from Hulme—who within a limited circle was acquiring some prestige as a theorist of the modern in poetry. But Hulme was not nearly so well known a critic as Hueffer, nor was he as close to Pound; Hueffer's insistence was probably a stimulus to Pound's revision of the weaknesses of his early manner, and, if it is necessary to account further for the crystallization of specific ideas into Imagism, the Hueffer relationship would explain this more satisfactorily than the one with Pound.

While it is clear that Pound's Imagism is similar to Hulme's in many important respects, it is not fair to dismiss Pound or his Imagism as under the "influence" of Hulme. He named his school hastily and not very seriously, as a means of drawing attention first to H. D.'s verse, then to any verse having the qualities he desired. He borrowed the name from Hulme because he was at the time interested in Hulme's theories and because these theories, at least in general, seemed to cover adequately the values of H.D.'s poems and, what is just as important, to coincide with what he was hearing about poetry from those he most respected, men like Hueffer and Yeats. It should be remembered that for both Hulme and Pound the image was a means to a more general end, good writing, and that an imagist poetry was only a logical way of insisting upon the freshness of language, the conciseness and economy necessary to achieving this end.

Hulme was an able exponent of his own theories, and his theories were persuasive because they articulated what other perceptive artists of the time thought and felt and often said but could formulate less pointedly. It is not unlikely that Pound may have owed something to Hulme for his realization of the importance of image and metaphor in a verse that might find acceptance in this century, that would correct the weaknesses of Romantic and Victorian poetry. But he was obviously not closely acquainted with or interested in the metaphysical basis for Hulme's aesthetic and ignored the detailed characteristics of the Hulme image, notably its ironic tone, evolving instead a definition consistent with his own concept of poetry. The principles of Pound's Imagism were simply the essentials of effective poetic expression as he had seen them in his studies, as he had discussed them on many occasions with Yeats and Hueffer—but summed up in a catchy and suggestive word or label he had heard from Hulme, who sought for poetry qualities similar to those Pound desired, who was said to be "a theorist with no more than a sort of scientific gift for discovery."

Pound did Hulme justice by publishing his poems at the close of *Ripostes*—Hulme was also an "Imagiste"—and the importance of Hulme is in his prediction of a course modern poetry would take, beginning as early as the Imagist movement. Since it was Pound who had access to the magazines which would give his ideas currency, since he was responsible for bringing to an imagistic poetry some measure of public notice, he appears justified in claiming for himself the credit for focusing the attention of his generation on the image in poetry, especially since the focus he gave it was his own. Several reasons might be given, then, for Pound's interest in the image—his own tastes in poetry, the techniques he noted in the poetry of Dante and the troubadours, of Rimbaud and certain of the French Symbolists, the theory and verse of Hulme, the qualities achieved by H. D.'s poems, and, not least, the growing awareness (in his own terms) of the real possibilities inherent in the label he had somewhat casually applied to verse which he hoped thus to publicize.

Circumstances provided other examples of Imagism and convinced him further of what his doctrine could do for poetry. Late in 1913 or early in 1914, he had become literary executor for the estate of Ernest Fenollosa. A portion of Fenollosa's research had been published in his *Epochs of Chinese and Japanese Art,* but at his death many of his notes, including decipherings of poems and plays into English, remained unedited. Pound began his work with the material on the Japanese "Noh" drama; his first publication of this material consisted of the translations from the "Noh" appearing in *Poetry* for May, 1914. By November, he had gone on to the Chinese poems, which drew admiring comment from H. D. ("Ezra is doing Chinese translations— and some are very beautiful! He comes running in four or five times a day now with new versions for us to read.")— in spite of her desire to keep clear of Pound and his Vorticist activities. For his part, Pound stated the importance of the Oriental literatures with customary emphasis.

The first step of a renaissance, or awakening, is the importation of models for painting, sculpture, or writing. . . . The last century rediscovered the middle ages. It is possible that this century may find a new Greece in China. In the meantime we have come upon a new table of values.[35]

And in quick succession he published three books which would demonstrate these values.[36]

He was not slow in drawing a parallel between Chinese and Imagist poetry. Fletcher says that by the summer of 1914 Pound was explaining Imagism in terms that involved the ideogram. The comparison, of course, did his movement no harm; but he was soon to be dropped from his own school as its members turned to Amy Lowell, even as he began to study material which made him ever more convinced of the soundness of the school's principles as he had established them.

As Fenollosa analyzed the Chinese written character, its relation to the image and to the Image (a further source of confusion) was immediately apparent, so apparent that Pound called him a forerunner of "modes of thought since fruitful" in Western painting and poetry. "The later movements in art have corroborated his theories."[37] He defined Chinese poetry as "a verbal medium consisting largely of semipictorial appeals to the eye," the appeals deriving from the fact that the written character, or ideogram, is based not on sound but on form; the word is really a picture of an

[35] "The Renaissance," *Poetry*, Vol. V, No. 5 (February, 1915), 228.
[36] *Cathay* (1915); *Certain Noble Plays of Japan* (1916); *"Noh," or Accomplishment* (1917).
[37] *Instigations* (New York, 1920), 357.

object or an operation in nature.[38] For example, the ideogram for *man* roughly resembles the object it represents. That for *sees* is more elaborate, a picture of a process, an eye moving through space. Fenollosa explained the character as follows: "a bold figure represented by running legs under an eye, a modified picture of an eye, a modified picture of running legs but unforgettable once you have seen it. . . . In reading Chinese, we do not seem to be juggling mental counters but to be watching *things* work out their own fate."

While the nature of the ideogram thus makes inevitable a poetry of vivid pictures, there is a still closer relation to Imagism. Although the ideogram is literal and pictorial, it can also represent "spiritual suggestions." This it does by "the use of material images to suggest immaterial relations," by use of metaphor. In an article of his own on the subject, Pound cited an example of the ideogram as metaphor: to convey the meaning equivalent to *ramble* or *visit*, the Chinese picture a king and a dog sitting in the stern of a boat. Here as elsewhere, language is informed with the strength of natural object and process. As Pound pointed out, the translator of Chinese has constantly to be on guard against canceling the verbal undertones and concreteness by the abstract words with which the English language abounds; he is dealing with a language which is strong and direct, and the Image or complex produced by this language will be strong and direct.[39] Pound had discovered further confirmation of his belief in the necessity for concreteness and natural strength in the poem.

His translations, or more exactly, his adaptations of Fen-

[38] Ernest Fenollosa, "An Essay on the Chinese Written Character as a Medium for Poetry," *Instigations*, 361–63.

ollosa's translations to English poetry, resulted in verse that is similar to that he used in illustration of Imagism—and further solidified what Pound had seemed to imply with his illustrations, the idea that an Imagist poem was brief, limited in meaning to what could be suggested by a vivid imagery of the physical, the natural. In fact, four of the six poems which he contributed to *Des Imagistes* were adaptations from the Chinese. "Fan-Piece, for Her Imperial Lord" and "Ts'ai Chi'h," which follow the *hokku* form that was the model for "In a Station of the Metro," are Imagistic by Pound's standards, and "Liu Ch'e" shows a similar technique in a slightly longer poem. The language is pictorial and close to the object or natural process; it does not degenerate into fuzzy abstractions and "literary" diction, for its meaning is anchored to the concrete object. It employs the image alone and occasionally as part of an analogy. While the poems extend awareness beyond the world of sense perception, Pound was willing to ignore this for the sake of surface beauty and precision. His specific statement on the question was made with reference to the "Noh," but applies as well to the poems of *Cathay*.

All through the winter of 1914 15 I watched Mr. Yeats correlating folklore . . . and data of the occult writers, with the habits of charlatans of Bond Street. If the Japanese authors had not combined the psychology of such matters with what is to me a very fine sort of poetry, I would not bother about it.[40]

[39] Pound's notes on the Fenollosa essay refer the reader to Aristotle on metaphor and to Pound on Vorticism; see pp. 376, 378. "But the greatest thing by far is to have a command of metaphor. This alone cannot be imparted by another; it is the mark of genius, for to make good metaphors implies an eye for resemblances."—*Aristotle*, trans. by S. H. Butcher (London, 1911), 87.

[40] *"Noh," or Accomplishment* (London, 1917), 44.

In the "Noh" drama, too, Pound discovered confirmation of his theory about the Image. Though he felt that the plays lacked the "solidity" of the translations from Rihaku, he declared that they had "Unity of Image," that is, their emotional pattern was concentrated in the associations evoked by a central, concrete figure: red maple leaves, pines, a snow flurry, or blue-gray waves. The structure of the Japanese play interested him, he said, because it paralled the structure sought in an *Imagiste* poem, which again raised the question of the length of such a poem. According to Pound's definition of the Image, length of the poem or Image is determined solely by the writer's ability to sustain a unified impression, to develop complexity as well as maintain unity of pattern or impact; and in his remarks on the "Noh" drama he asserted it should be defined only in this way.

Several months after he received the Fenollosa papers, he became involved in Wyndham Lewis' Vorticist movement. Two of the principal theories on which the Vorticists insisted underlined the concerns Pound developed from his own early studies, from Hulme and from his work with the Oriental literatures. One was the necessity for a vigorous aesthetic impact ("The vortex is the point of maximum energy."), which parallels his praise of the Chinese for the strength it derives from its verbal undertones. The other is the belief that the image is the "primary pigment" of poetry, the extreme of emphasis to which his theorizing about the Image was drawn.

Every concept, every emotion presents itself to the vivid consciousness in some primary form. It belongs to the art of this form. If sound, to music; if formed words, to literature; the image, to poetry; form, to design; colour in position, to paint-

*ing; form or design in three planes, to sculpture; movement, to
the dance or to the rhythm of music or verses.*[41]

Here he uses the term in its conventional sense, as the single,
verbal reproduction of a sense impression, which makes it
clear that the Image, for Pound, depended upon the image;
but as Vorticist he also explained that a long Imagist poem
is possible because the Image is a vortex "from which, and
through which, and into which, ideas are constantly rush-
ing"—and Image may mean either the single verbal element, the metaphor which involves two images, or the total
impact of a poem, with the suggestion that this has a visual
basis, presents a definite picture, and will itself be metaphor,
making the intangible concrete.

In 1918 Pound remarked to Harriet Monroe that "language" was what had made all of his work since "Contemporania" interesting. If Imagism was his search for the essence of the poetic, it was also an ideal he could not expect
to reach with every attempt, and many of the poems written
during the 1912–17 period are experiments in a different
vein. On "The Temperaments," he commented: "You may
not like it, but even W. B. Y. who for the most part detests
my lighter vein, admits that HERE I have the true quality,
the real, the hellenic epigram." Martial and the epigram-
matists of the Greek anthology have been suggested as
models for this lighter vein, and there are also obvious resemblances to Catullus;[42] but the point to be made here is
that these poems, often of biting social comment, further
illustrate the effort Pound was making to expunge the "lit-

---

[41] "Vortex," *Blast*, Vol. I, No. 1 (June 20, 1914), 153.

[42] T. S. Eliot, *Ezra Pound: His Metric & His Poetry* (New York,
1917), *xviii.*

erary" and the conventionalized from his verse. Like Imagism, but in a different way, they were part of his aim to bring poetry up to the level of prose, to discover a language appropriate to his time. The technique of the Mauberly sequence profits by both kinds of experiment; but their importance to his development may be seen best in his major project, the *Cantos*, the first three of which he published in 1917—and in both poems he is still the seeker after a strong, clear-edged beauty (of Venus, not Eros), whose energies radiate from a form he designated as Imagism.

VII

"Amygism"

AFTER the late summer of 1914, Pound's statements about Imagism lacked authority. Although he continued to support its doctrine, the publication of *Some Imagist Poets* in 1915 made Amy Lowell's leadership an accomplished fact. Under his guidance, Imagism had been at once a specific creed and a rather subjective yardstick which he could apply to any poetry that attracted his notice. Under Amy Lowell, it stood for certain carefully explained principles, and, whatever their shortcomings, those principles were immediately accepted as the definitive statement of doctrinaire Imagism.

The revised doctrine was announced in the prefaces to the anthologies of 1915 and 1916. Like the *Poetry* manifesto, its statements are general in nature and require documentation from the writings of those who were chiefly responsible for them. For a time after Miss Lowell suddenly assumed the sponsorship of the movement, she tactfully relied on Aldington for her understanding of its aims. H. D. was no theorist, and Lawrence and Fletcher had not been associated with Pound's original program; Flint could have helped her and without doubt did to some extent, but it was on Aldington that she chiefly depended. While she asserted that all six of the contributors had a hand in the prefaces, they were largely a synthesis of her ideas and of his. It is through Aldington's critical comment first that one approaches the Imagism of the prefaces.

An article which he contributed to *The Egoist* for June, 1914, offers a satisfactory point of departure.[1] In it he gave more elaborate and detailed explanation of Imagism than anyone had yet attempted, including not only the principles of the *Poetry* manifesto, but others which had merely been mentioned in the course of miscellaneous critical articles. Since the new principles were later incorporated into the prefaces and thus became official doctrine, Aldington's article provides an interesting transition between the program of 1913 and that upon which the poets finally agreed.

Like Pound, he placed considerable emphasis upon the kind of poetic language for which Imagism stood. The Imagists, he said use as few adjectives as possible. Though stated as a separate principle, this related to another, perhaps more important:

> The exact word. We make quite a heavy stress on that. . . . All great poetry is exact. All the dreariness of nineteenth century poets comes from their not quite knowing what they wanted to say and filling up the gaps with portentous adjectives and idiotic similes.

Elsewhere, Aldington added a further note to his concept of the diction appropriate to modern poetry. He described its aim as "speakable English" and recommended that the poet observe this simple rule: syntax or vocabulary unsuit-

[1] "Modern Poetry and the Imagists," *The Egoist*, Vol. I, No. 11 (June 1, 1914), 201–203.

able to prose has no place in poetry. For another *Egoist* article he illustrated both good and bad diction by quoting a passage from the verse of H. D. In three lines otherwise stylistically perfect he objected to one word, *meads*, on the ground that it is a stock "poetic" word which would not be used in prose statement.

Aldington also shared Pound's admiration for the quality of "hardness" in poetry; the second of the principles he listed in "Modern Poetry and the Imagists" demanded of a poem a "hardness, as of cut stone. No slop, no sentimentality." His poems show a feeling for the beauty of natural objects, the human body, or physical passions, which he found best expressed through the art and mythology of classical Greece. For example, in "To a Greek Marble" he recreates the intense reaction to physical beauty which must have moved the sculptor of this piece; in "Choricos" he personifies death as a cold, chaste woman who brings rest and forgetfulness.

He did not confine his attention entirely to classical subjects, but when he turned to contemporary scenes he could not always adequately objectify his attitude toward them. Neither "Childhood," which describes the dull, grimy town in which he was reared, nor "Eros and Psyche," which argues the incongruity of these figures in a modern industrial city, is successful poetic statement because the poet never transcends his personal distaste for his material. Nor were other attempts to draw material from the scenes around him completely satisfactory. *"Au Vieux Jardin,"* a poem in the manner of H. D., offers the poet's reaction to the rose and white colors of smooth flagstones and the pale, yellow grasses growing between them. The spectacle of a man so affected by the appearance of a blade of grass provoked rather unsympathetic comments from some critics, as Aldington fully realized: "I shall not be unwilling to counteract the somewhat 'precious' effect of the poems I have published in Poetry and that infernal Glebe anthology."

Aldington's interpretation of Imagism did not ignore matters more specifically Imagistic. At the head of his list of principles was "Direct treatment of the subject. . . . We convey an emotion by presenting the object and circumstances of that emotion without comment." Instead of using "twenty-five" adjectives to describe a woman, the Imagist presents her in an image. Thus Aldington, too, understood direct treatment as dependent upon the image; and he stated his conviction that the title of the movement appropriately reflected its basic doctrine.

I think it [*Des Imagistes*] a very good and descriptive title, and it serves to enunciate some of the principles we most firmly believe in. It cuts us away from the "cosmic" crowd and it equally bars us off from the "abstract art" gang, and it annoys quite a lot of fools.

His use of the image does not permit dogmatic conclusions about what it meant to him. All one can safely say is that his theory and practice were similar to those of Pound: Imagism centered upon the image, but the image was not limited by Hulme's definition of it. "To A Greek Marble" presents a succession of images which make not only pictorial, but aural and tactile appeals: fragile pipes, cicada song, brown fingers moving over slim shoulders, the "sun upon thy breasts." The poem does not rely upon metaphor but bases its appeal upon the cumulative effect of a succession of separate images. Aldington, however, also employed imagery in another manner recommended by Pound: by sudden and apt comparison to communicate "an intellectual and emotional complex in an instant of time."

> *The blue smoke leaps*
> *Like swirling clouds of birds, vanishing.*
> *So my love leaps toward you,*
> *Vanishes and is renewed.*

Or

> *She has new leaves*
> *After her dead flowers,*
> *Like the little almond tree*
> *Which the frost hurt.*[2]

Short poems like these, in which simile or metaphor is the basis for communication achieve a hardness and objectivity that would have suited Pound, if not Hulme. Only occasionally did Aldington create an image that in all respects fits Hulme's definition.

> *The chimneys rank on rank,*
> *Cut the clear sky;*
> *The moon*
> *With a rag of gauze about her loins,*
> *Poses among them, an awkward Venus—*

And

> *At night, the moon, a pregnant woman,*
> *Walks cautiously over the slippery heavens.*[3]

[2] "Images, II," *Collected Poems* (New York, 1929), 20; "New Love," *Some Imagists Poets* (1915), 15.

[3] "Evening," "London (May, 1915)," *Collected Poems*, 32, 37.

There is other evidence that Aldington's thinking had been affected by Hulme's ideas. In 1918, he objected to the omission of Hulme's name from the dedication of an anthology to the "gallant gentlemen," contributors to the arts, who lost their lives during the war, saying: "Hulme had considerable influence at one time among the younger men."[4] Two years later, his "Art of Poetry" employed language clearly reminiscent of Hulme:

Poetry has no place for mere intellectual counters . . . the dead metaphor, . . . Look for the phrases that give one a sudden shock of illumination, which really evoke an object or convey a sensation.[5]

And he apparently accepted Flint's statements about the history of Imagism, yet his single remark on the image was decidedly at odds with Hulme's concept: "We wanted to write hard, clear patterns of words, interpreting moods by 'images,' i. e., by pictures, *not* similes."[6]

Aldington's view of Imagism, though much more detailed, repeats to the letter the view presented by Pound's *Poetry* manifesto; it even includes Pound's "Don'ts" as doctrinaire Imagism. They further agreed in rejecting Symbolism. Referring to a book by De Gourmont, Aldington noted: "by a Symbolist, and *that* won't take," though he later tempered this attitude to a certain extent: "We . . . disliked the cosmic, the Bridges-like, the Masefieldian, the Georgian and the Symbolists (these last we tolerated)."[7]

[4] "New Paths," *The Dial*, Vol. LXV, No. 772 (September 5, 1918), 150.

[5] *The Dial*, Vol. LXIX, No. 2 (August, 1920), 169–70.

[6] Letter (unpublished) to Amy Lowell, November 10, 1917.

In fact, Aldington's influence was (while Pound was carry-ing Imagism to extremes) a conservative one, keeping the movement to the moderate but fairly well-defined route on which it began.

We, the Imagists, set out to do something definite for English poetry, to correct certain tendencies, and to foster others. . . . When we publish our own books we publish as *individuals* and are individually responsible, but in the anthology we publish as a group, and if that grouping is to be artistically effective, we must *strictly* adhere to our programme. . . . Let us write and publish our experiments by all means, but not in the anthology.[8]

Yet he tended to see Imagist doctrine as a set of prin-ciples whose value resided in their cumulative effect rather than in the critical concept of the image. Of the tenets on which the present discussion has been based, he said: "You will see that they are all practically stylistic." And when he explained the movement for the *Bruno Chap Books,* he spoke in even more general terms.

What then is Imagism? Briefly, it is an ideal of style, an at-tempt to recreate in our language and for our time a poetry that shall have the qualities of the great poetry of old. . . . Imagists seek the qualities that make Sappho, Catullus, Villon, the French Symbolists (whose influence still dominates all European poetry) great.[9]

[7] "Modern Poetry and the Imagists," *The Egoist,* Vol. I, No. 11 (June 1, 1914), 201; letter to Amy Lowell, January 18, 1916.

[8] Letter to Amy Lowell, January 18, 1916.

[9] "The Imagists," *Bruno Chap Books,* Special Series No. 5, Vol. II (1915), 69, 70.

In so describing the school, he was continuing a tendency apparent in comments by most of the Imagists at one time or another. Pound had called it a movement concerned with criticism, rather than creation—an attempt to bring poetry up to the level of prose.

Amy Lowell carried the generalizing tendency to its logical extreme: Imagism under her guidance became so inclusive that it was less a specific doctrine than a platform designed to win the approval of almost anyone interested in honest, sincere poetic technique. This is not to say that she had no clearly definable theory; in some respects her thinking about the problems of modern poetry was more conscientious and better organized than Pound's or Aldington's, but several of her conclusions are incompatible with those on which Imagism was originally based. She made some effort to keep within the bounds prescribed for the movement; but Imagism never successfully modified certain of her convictions, and these convictions were simply not those of Hulme, Pound, or Aldington.

Her views on the language of poetry are a case in point. She condemned the use of inversions and of locutions inappropriate to the diction of natural, conversational prose; she also asserted the importance of the exact word. Her "exact word," however, was not the one which describes a thing as it is, but the one which most effectively communicates the writer's impression of it. In illustration, she quoted:

> Great heaps of shining glass
> Pricked out of the stubble
> By a full, high moon.[10]

[10] *Tendencies in Modern American Poetry* (Boston and New York, 1931), 242.

Though she meant to emphasize the use of *glass* to convey the writer's impression of stones or pebbles in this picture, *pricked out* could also serve as an example. Again in "Venus Transiens," trying to give her impression of a Botticelli painting, she described his waves as *crinkled*. Like Hueffer's Impressionist, Miss Lowell aimed to "render," not merely to report, and while her theory of diction begins as Imagist, it trails off into Impressionism.

She placed no particular stress upon the "hardness" of good poetry; but her strictures upon subject matter approximate the doctrine of Aldington and Pound and offer a pair of terms which, though too general to be final, shed further light on the Imagist position.[11] One was *internality*, "the most marked quality in the poetry of the nineties." Whether or not the term accurately characterizes the poetic attitude of the nineties, Miss Lowell was quite certain of what it meant to her. She referred to the pathetic fallacy, the view of nature as important only for its reflection of the poet's mood, as of no interest apart from the individual; and she criticized this view for its assumption that man is the center of the universe, a criticism that is by now familiar enough.

In contrast, she saw modern poetry as characterized by externality or exteriority, by "a contemplation of nature unencumbered by the 'pathetic fallacy.'" Externality encourages an "interest in things for themselves and not because of the effect they have on oneself." She pointed, for example, to the modern artist's handling of colors, light, and shade, "with practically no insistence on the substances which pro-

[11] For her use of these terms, see "The New Manner in Modern Poetry," *The New Republic*, Vol. VI, No. 70 (March 4, 1916), 124; *Six French Poets* (New York, 1916), 215; "A Consideration of Modern Poetry," *The North American Review*, Vol. CCV, No. 734 (January, 1917), 106.

duce them, be they men or houses or trees or water." A product of the sensible attitude which sees man in his proper, relatively insignificant place in the universe, externality would not seem to encourage introspection, though she was not willing wholly to exclude it from poetry. Her theory is of some importance because it again draws attention to the very broad but basic difference between the impersonal art of Hulme and Pound on the one hand and the subjective, egocentric art of Symbolism on the other. While not necessarily derived from Hulme, it is a clear, if generalized and unphilosophical, echo of the principles underlying his aesthetic.

But she also discussed poetry in the exact terms Hulme had hoped to do away with. She declared that poetry consists of two ingredients, the vision and the words. When the vision is slight, it calls *fancy* into play; when its force is stronger, it finds expression through the *imagination;* when it carries the poet before it, it has become *inspiration.* She even stated that the dominant quality of the modern idiom (in which she included Imagism) was suggestion, "the invoking of a place or a character rather than describing it, . . . the implying of something rather than the stating of it, implying it perhaps under a metaphor, perhaps in an even less obvious way."[12] By supporting this assertion with two examples from Fletcher's poetry, she brought her definition to what is approximately the position of the Symbolist. On one she commented: "The picture as given is quite clear and vivid. But the picture we see is not the poem, the real poem lies beyond, is only suggested." On the other: "This

[12] "A Consideration of Modern Poetry," *The North American Review*, Vol. CCV, No. 734 (January, 1917), 103–104; *Tendencies in Modern American Poetry*, 247.

is at once Mr. Fletcher and Japan. It is brief and clear, and
the suggestion never becomes statement, but floats, a nimbus,
over the short, sharp lines."[13]

However, Miss Lowell, from her own statements, was
not a Symbolist; she considered Symbolist poetry "beautiful," but saw in it too much "internality," too much of the
poet's "inner self."[14] Although her "Patterns" is symbolism,
its concrete, vivid images (the garden paths, the brocaded
gown, the rigid stays) symbolizing the human patterns and
conventions that cut across the natural desires of the individual, it is what one might call a symbolism of externality.
The Symbolists sought to communicate an "internal" meaning and used the symbol, among other devices, to heighten
the mystery of the inexpressible; Miss Lowell dealt with
the expressible, or with a tension very simple in nature; her
poem expresses a state of consciousness, but it is an elementary and uncomplicated one having and making no claim
to reproduction of the quality of consciousness itself—and
her symbols are turned in the direction of making the expressible more concrete.

If she was not a Symbolist, neither was she an Imagist.
Her concept of the image was so vague as to be meaningless.
It is true that she did not completely ignore the function of
the image in poetry: she accepted Hulme as the original
Imagist, and her preface to *Sword Blades* explains that in
order to give the reader some poignant feeling he has had,
the poet must find new images, old ones, like *daybreak*, having been so overworked that they have lost their pictorial
effectiveness. She recognized that vividness, the throwing
of "an inescapable picture" on the mind's eye, was one of

[13] *Tendencies in Modern American Poetry*, 247, 341.
[14] *Six French Poets*, 215.

the dominant qualities of modern poetry, and pointed out the way in which this tends to encourage a concentration of poetic effect and discourage what Pound called hanging the image "with festoons."[15] Like other moderns, she could create a brilliant visual image:

> *Grass-blades push up between the cobblestones*
> *And catch the sun on their flat sides*
> *Shooting it back,*
> *Gold and emerald*
> *Into the eyes of passers-by.*[16]

However, she seldom tried to use an image in metaphor or simile, and what efforts she made in this direction were not always successful. "Bullion" describes the poet's thoughts "chinking" against his ribs like "silver hail stones," and, even if the reader accepts the idea that the thoughts are those emanating from the heart and that they may therefore not illogically chink against the ribs, the connotations of *chinking* and *hailstones*, even silver ones, are not appropriate to the emotion with which the poet is concerned. At the same time, a more successful use of a metaphor should be pointed out. Seeking to transcribe her impression of a composition by Stravinsky, Miss Lowell translates the music first into the heavy, uneven clomp of wooden shoes on slippery cobblestones, then into the cacophonous rattle of bones, a grotesque sound—"Delirium flapping its thighbones."[17]

What has been implied by the discussion so far is clearly

[15] "A Consideration of Modern Poetry," *The North American Review*, Vol. CCV, No. 734 (January, 1917), 105.

[16] "The Traveling Bear," *Some Imagist Poets* (1915), 83.

[17] "Stravinsky's Three Pieces, 'Grotesque' for String Quartet," *Some Imagist Poets* (1916), 88.

given away in her statements about the Imagist movement. The doctrine of the image, she said, "refers more to the manner of presentation than to the thing presented"; and she summarized the Imagist credo without reference to it:

Simplicity and directness of speech; subtlety and beauty of rhythms; individualistic freedom of idea; clearness and vividness of presentation; and concentration. Not new principles, by any means . . . but fallen into desuetude.[18]

A symbolist without the philosophical attitude of Symbolism and an Imagist without the image, she carried to its extreme a tendency to generalize Imagist principles until they ignored the tenet which presumably gave the doctrine its individuality and its name.

A word about the poetry of John Gould Fletcher will indicate the inclusiveness of "Amygism." Fletcher understood the principles upon which doctrinaire Imagism had originally been based. In *The Little Review*, he cited four cardinal beliefs as the basis for the movement, the first being to "present the subject as an image," so that the reader may re-enact for himself the "emotional complex" the poet is trying to convey. He warned against confusing Imagist aims with those of the nineteenth-century Symbolists, and drew a further, equally just, distinction between Imagism and *vers libre:* "Imagism is an attitude of mind that can appear just as easily in rime."[19]

Fletcher had refused to contribute to *Des Imagistes.* When the *Poetry* manifesto was published in 1913, he stated

[18] *Tendencies in Modern American Poetry,* 246–47.
[19] "Three Imagist Poets," *The Little Review,* Vol. III, No. 3 (May, 1916), 30–31.

to Harriet Monroe his disapproval of the school, as such, rather than of the principles for which the school stood.

With Mr. Pound's "school" of "Imagisme," I am in even greater disagreement. "Imagisme" is an attitude towards technique, pure and simple. I am unable, and I wish everyone else were unable, to impose upon myself the pedantic yoke of any particular technique. . . . I have informed Mr. Pound that I do not intend to hamper myself with his technique and his "don'ts."

Because of the *New Age* series on the French poets, Fletcher's attitude towards Pound was not, at the moment, friendly; but their relationship soon grew more cordial, and he wrote for Pound what he considered an Imagist poem. Still, he would not make the public declaration which appearance in *Des Imagistes* would have implied. Amy Lowell, on the other hand, completely won his confidence. He accepted the invitation to join her group, but the association was an uneasy one.

Fletcher's major effort during the years to 1917 was a series of "Symphonies," which were to present important phases in the intellectual and emotional development of an artist. Each phase was to be symbolized by a color, each color evoking in the poet's mind certain pictures which were to impress the desired emotional and imaginative effect upon the reader.

I have tried to state each phase in the terms of a certain color, or combination of colors which is emotionally akin to that phase. This color, and the imaginative phantasmagoria of landscape which it evokes, thereby creates, in a definite and tangible form, the dominant mood of each poem.

The "Blue Symphony" deals with the young artist's search for beauty; confused at first by his own immaturity and by the influence of other men, he finally attains self-assurance through recognition that the vision which he pursues will always elude him. The color *blue* was suggested to Fletcher by the emotions accompanying perception of mystery, depth, distance—emotions which he thought appropriate to the theme; at the same time, it evoked in his mind the specific images of mist, smoke, death-mountains, which would stimulate these emotions in the reader. To heighten the effect of unreality, Fletcher introduced his imagery in the logically unrelated pattern characteristic of certain poems by Rimbaud.

The "White Symphony" follows a pattern that resembles the Rimbaud technique even more closely. The title of the poem recalls Gautier's *"Symphonie en blanc majeur"*; its "symphonic" progression (by sections or movements, each developing a mood through its color symbolism) also derives, in some measure, from the possibilities suggested by the title of the French poem. However, its theme, the struggle for the inaccessible, the eternal, is neither Parnassian nor Imagist, and its use of *white* to symbolize this absolute repeats a Symbolist device. Its images, products of the hallucinatory imagination, directed by the subconscious, resemble the phantasmagoria of *Les Illuminations*. In the opening passage, for example, white petals of peonies thrust out to embrace the onlooker, thrust out until they lose their identity and are transformed first into flakes of snow, then the dazzling white of clouds; the transition from one image to the next is handled in such a way as to recreate the "impossible" behavior of images in dreams.

Fletcher, in fact, develops his imagery from the correspondences for E (white—mists, lancelike glaciers, etc.) and for O (blue—Omega, silences of the heavens) indicated by Rimbaud in his "Vowels" sonnet—"White Symphony" moving from the radiance of the ecstasy in section I to the blue of the eternal in section II and back to white in section III, now the pallor of death as the human dream fails. In the "Symphonies," Fletcher tries to state each mood, through his color imagery, in terms the reader can see or feel, and the poems have little meaning in the conventional sense: to this extent they are Imagistic (as are the Japanese poems which interested Fletcher and Amy Lowell, as well as Pound). Yet they make assumptions which Imagism, at least implicitly, denies; they deal with the imprecise—no matter how precisely—and go beyond the Imagist's tendency to make language more scientific and precise, its almost naturalistic tendency to confine expression within the limits of the solid, physical sensation or feeling.

Fletcher used this technique in poetry that was to be Imagistic. "Blue Symphony," again with its *long-O* words to establish the correspondences suggested by Rimbaud, was written as an Imagist poem; "London Excursion," which employs the same "unrelated" method of progression, was also published in the anthology of 1915. Its attempt to communicate a reaction to the modern city is not inconsistent with Imagism, because the poet sees no transcendental significance in his object. Its method, however, is not to bring the reader closer to the object that he may react to it or see it more clearly as it is, but to interpose the poet's quite subjective impressions of the scene. The images are wholly impressionistic, and their final effect derives from the strangeness and individuality of the poet's view; being one significant step removed from reality, they lose the hard-

ness and objectivity of Imagism: domes of bowler hats
vibrate in the heat, the city seems to throw its streets after
those who flee from it.

Certain descriptive poems that Fletcher contributed to
the anthologies demonstrate other characteristics not inconsistent with Imagism. For example, they reveal his ability
to depict color vividly:

> *Shadows of blue hands passing*
> *Over a curtain of flame.*
>
> *Grey rain curtains wave afar off,*
> *Wisps of vapor curl and vanish.*
> *The sun throws soft shades of golden light*
> *Over rose-buttressed palisades.*
>
> *Now the clouds are a lazy procession,*
> *Blue balloons bobbing solemnly*
> *Over black-dappled walls.*[20]

On occasion, he could create an image like that advocated
by Hulme. He wrote of "The Unquiet Street":

> *On rainy nights*
> *It dully gleams*
> *Like the cold tarnished scales of a snake;*
> *And over it hang arc-lamps,*
> *Blue-white death lilies on black stems.*

Or

> *And the grinding click of their skates as they*
> *impinge on the surface*

[20] "Clouds Across the Canyon," *Some Imagist Poets* (1916), 40, 41.

*Is like the brushing together of their wing-tips
of silver.*[21]

Such imagery, however, is so rare as to pass unnoticed in his predominantly Symbolist technique, and would not seem to justify his inclusion in Imagist volumes. Privately, to Amy Lowell, Fletcher admitted the anomaly of his association with the three anthologies.

I do not believe that a poem should present an "image," I believe it should present an emotion. I do not believe in "clear, hard, and definite presentation." I believe in a complete, that is to say, shifting and fluid presentation. I do not believe in "absolute freedom in choice of subject."—I believe that the very word "choice" means lack of freedom. If one chooses, one has certain standards whereby one chooses. I do not believe that the "exact word" is possible. I do not believe in cadence, but in rhythm (a different thing altogether). I do not believe altogether in "externality." Therefore I do not accept Imagism. I am a Rhythmist or a Symbolist, but not an Imagist.

It is little wonder that the prefaces, accepted as the official statement of doctrinaire Imagism, consist of broad and disappointingly unrevolutionary principles.[22] How otherwise could they present a program upon which there was a reasonable semblance of agreement among poets of such diverse techniques; how otherwise could they reconcile the assumptions of Imagist and Symbolist? Of course, they incline toward the beliefs of those who wrote them, toward the

[21] "The Skaters," *Some Imagist Poets* (1916), 48.
[22] See *Some Imagist Poets* (1915), Preface, *v–vii*; *Some Imagist Poets* (1916), Preface, *v–xi*.

ideas of Aldington and Amy Lowell; but they had, nevertheless, in some measure to cover the practice of a poet
like Fletcher, who refused to join Pound's group and who
even repudiated (though in private) the generalities of
"Amygism."

In addition to being general, the prefaces stand in ques-
tionable relationship to the theories of T. E. Hulme and
even to those of Pound. Damon writes: "The derivation
from Hulme is obvious. . . . The difference from the epi-
grams of *Speculations* is chiefly the result of the arguments
and experiments of many persons over a number of years.
The Imagist credo of 1915 is the sifting out of his theories
and the reduction to essentials."[23] One recalls, however,
that Hulme was not widely known, not nearly so respected
a figure, for example, as Hueffer. He recalls, too, that
Pound, who originated the movement, borrowed only the
most superficial aspects of Hulme's theory, and that Aldington, who also attended the meetings on Frith Street, shows
little evidence of having been influenced by any explanation
of Imagism but Pound's. Flint and Fletcher, though both
acquainted with Hulme and relatively unaffected by Pound's
criticism, developed a theory and practice which does not
resemble the doctrine preached by either. Thus Amy Lowell, who did not know Hulme, would have had to take her
knowledge of his work not only at second hand but from
poets who did not fully understand or sympathize with what
he was trying to do; and, while she submitted for a time
to Pound's supervision, she soon asserted her independence
and her right to interpret the movement in her own way.

The prefaces devote more attention to stating a belief
in free verse than to any other principle.

23 *Amy Lowell*, 303.

To create new rhythms—as the expression of new moods—and not to copy old rhythms, which merely echo old moods. We do not insist upon "free-verse" as the only method of writing poetry. We fight for it as for a principle of liberty. We believe that the individuality of a poet may often be better expressed in free-verse than in conventional forms. In poetry, a new cadence means a new idea.

Two points are worth mention. The idea of free verse is obviously attributed to the French: the language of the first and last sentences is that of Duhamel and Vildrac, who, with the Greek Melic poets and with other French writers on metrics, are cited as Imagist sources. Moreover, *vers libre* has been given an official link with Imagism; Hulme recommended a free form, but he did not make the recommendation essential to Imagism; Pound recommended the musical phrase, but did not specify *vers libre*. The 1915 preface not only accepted *vers libre* as Imagistic but elevated it to a position of central importance in its doctrine. That Imagist attention was now fixed primarily upon the rhythms of poetry is further indicated by the explanation given this principle in the 1916 anthology: "Poetry is a spoken and not a written art."

The language principle also modified an earlier tenet: "To use the language of common speech, but to employ always the *exact* word, not the nearly-exact, nor the merely decorative word." Hulme discussed the necessity for the exact word and implied the need for a diction more natural than that commonly considered poetic; Pound's manifesto called only for elimination of the decorative word, though his other criticism involved the requirement that poetry be as exact as the best prose. The significant point occurs in the elaboration of the language principle published in the 1916 preface.

The "exact" word does not mean the word which exactly describes the object in itself, it means the "exact" word which brings the effect of that object before the reader as it presented itself to the poet's mind at the time of writing the poem.

This is not only Amy Lowell, but it is Amy Lowell advocating something like Hueffer's Impressionism. Since the exact word was apparently Hueffer's *mot juste;* since Hueffer's criticism also recommended use of colloquial, even vulgar, language in poetry; and since Pound, Aldington, and the rest held Hueffer in high regard, it seems just as reasonable to attribute this concept to his influence as to Hulme's.

A third principle is also familiar, but is less easily traced to a source: "To produce poetry that is hard and clear, never blurred nor indefinite." It clearly parallels Hulme's advice to the poet: dependence upon the natural object as the basis for analogy was supposed to create the quality of hardness; but hardness was also an aim of Impressionism as Hueffer interpreted it; one effect of "rendering" rather than reporting is that the impression which the poet gives will be hard, will remain with the reader. Pound also began to argue for hardness in poetry as early as 1911; since he never stated specifically what he meant by the word, it is difficult to say whether the idea, which appeared rather suddenly in his criticism, was his own, Hulme's, or Hueffer's. He was certainly closer to Hueffer and would have been more likely to accept advice from him. It is even possible that the idea may be traced to De Gourmont's *Le Problème du style,* which, as we know, the Imagists read with care. In any case, it was not a part of the *Poetry* manifesto, and its place in the prefaces seems due less to the influence of one individual than to the currency which a word will frequently achieve when it happens to be a felicitous expression of what many individuals more or less vaguely feel.

Two other principles are entirely new to Imagism. One involved subject matter.

To allow absolute freedom in the choice of subject. It is not good art to write badly about aeroplanes and automobiles; nor is it necessarily bad art to write well about the past. We believe passionately in the artistic value of modern life, but we wish to point out that there is nothing so uninspiring nor so old-fashioned as an aeroplane of the year 1911.

The imagery of the five poems by Hulme published in *Ripostes* may have implied that the artist should draw his material from modern life, but no such statement appears in his theory. It was Hueffer who exhorted the poet to render his own times and Pound who made the expression a catch-phrase of his criticism. However, the principle does not so much represent a borrowing of an idea as it does an assertion of freedom from any one narrow concept. The question of subject matter was a controversial one at the time; treatment of contemporary subjects was, for example, a cardinal principle of the Futurists, whose explosive antics rocked literary London in 1913. Had it not been for Futurism, to which every alert artist reacted in one way or another, the Imagist position on subject matter would probably not have required formal statement.

The other involved "concentration"; "most of us believe that concentration is of the very essence of poetry."

The word is traceable not to Hulme, Pound, or Hueffer, but to S. Foster Damon, who first applied it to Imagism. Amy Lowell found it a convenient way of expressing the modern desire to avoid "all blurring, extraneous detail"; with a nod to Damon, she incorporated *concentration* into her discussion of the modern idiom and, by including it in the 1915 preface, made it a part of the Imagist program.[24]

On the question of the image, the prefaces are enlightening by their very vagueness and ambiguity.

To present an image (hence the name: "Imagist"). We are not a school of painters, but we believe that poetry should render particulars exactly and not deal in vague generalities, however magnificent and sonorous. It is for this reason that we oppose the cosmic poet, who seems to us to shirk the real difficulties of his art.

While the statement, especially as it exorcises the cosmic in poetry, resembles Hulme's doctrine in a general way, it, too, apparently avoids explicit reference to the character of the image itself. The 1916 preface attempted to remedy the omission, and in so doing rejected Hulme's concept.

"Imagism" does not mean merely the presentation of pictures. "Imagism" refers to the manner of presentation, not to the subject. It means a clear presentation of whatever the author wishes to convey. He may wish to convey a mood of indecision, in which case the poem should be indecisive.

A theory which merely defines *image* as *clear presentation* has no legitimate claim to call itself Imagism. If Imagism

[24] "A Consideration of Modern Poetry," *The North American Review*, Vol. CCV, No. 734 (January, 1917), 106.

had not, as Pound insisted, gone "off into froth," it had undeniably lost the right to its name. The prefaces frankly acknowledged the orthodox and general nature of their creed: "These principles are not new; they have fallen into desuetude. They are the essentials of all great poetry, indeed of all great literature." In a sense, there was no "movement" or "school"—there were Hulme the theorist and Pound the theorist and practitioner, agreeing on certain important fundamentals, and there was a group of poets, more or less closely associated with them, whose creative efforts tended at some times and on some points to agree with their standards for a modern poetry.

VIII

Imagists, Vorticists, and Others

I MAGISM was only one expression of a far-reaching revolution in the arts. When the Imagist sought the public eye, he had to compete with the Futurist, the Vorticist, and the Post-Impressionist, to name only the more radical of the experimentalists. Each assumed the inadequacy of techniques previously admired and offered a program of revision; each strove to develop a doctrine that would take root in what was agreed to be the new soil of twentieth-century consciousness. As Wyndham Lewis, a Vorticist, said: "In every case the structural and philosophic rudiments of life were sought out. On all hands a return to first principles was witnessed."[1]

The Imagist poets were well aware of other doctrine. In "Imagisme," Flint had pointed out that the school was contemporary with Post-Impressionism and Futurism, but hastened to add that it had nothing in common with them. Aldington's comments also indicate a desire to keep Imagism free of the opprobrium that might attach to less dignified manifestations of artistic revolt; sending some work by H. D., he wrote Miss Monroe that it was contemporary with the Cubists and Vorticists without their eccentricities.

[1] *Blasting and Bombardiering* (London, 1937), 260–61.

187

Amy Lowell, in "The New Manner," carefully explained that *externality* was not meant to encourage what she called a "Futurist" treatment of subject matter. Pound, on the contrary, sought to relate his work to that of other modernisms: "These two latter sorts of poems ["Heather" and "The Return"] . . . are Imagisme, and in so far as they are Imagisme, they fall in with the new pictures and the new sculpture."[2]

It is possible that Pound's statement may have been simply an effort to borrow for his school some of the fire and brimstone associated with Vorticism and thus further *"épater les bourgeois"*; but it underlines the necessity for considering Imagism in relation to the aesthetic movements alongside which it developed. The present chapter will examine, specifically, the Imagist-Vorticist bond upon which Pound insisted, and, more generally, will outline certain similarities and differences among the leading schools; it will suggest, finally, that the philosophical attitude worked out by Hulme as a basis for his imagism may find a parallel in the fundamental assumptions of their aesthetics.

The first organized move in the war against outmoded techniques was the exhibition of Post-Impressionist painting held at the Grafton Galleries in 1911. Douglas Goldring places it alongside Futurism as one of the major excitements of the prewar years; John Cournos writes that it "was to open my eyes to the rising revolt of the artists against the bourgeoisie amidst the crucifying guffaws of the bourgeois public";[3] it finally decided Fletcher in favor of experiment in verse. Although a movement concerned

---

[2] "Vorticism," *The Fortnightly Review*, Vol. XCVI, No. dlxxiii (September 1, 1914), 464.

[3] *Autobiography*, 211.

exclusively with the visual arts, Post-Impressionism is of some relevance here not only because its impact was felt by all artists but because its tenets are representative of the trend taken by the art of which Hulme and Pound approved, an art which enlisted the sympathies of many English painters and critics.

Roger Fry, who arranged the Grafton exhibition, delivered a lecture at its close which provides a concise summary of its aims.[4] He expressed his objection to the standard which measures a work of art solely in terms of how accurately it reproduces the natural object and which considers Renaissance painting the nearest approach to perfection because it most successfully mirrors the external world. Since the artist cannot achieve a complete illusion of reality, representation should never be the sole aim of his art, and, as the history of art proves, it frequently has not been his primary aim.

Re-examining the aesthetic feeling, Fry argued for the Post-Impressionist that the most direct appeals to the imagination are not based upon recognition of likeness. Certain images, he insisted, have aesthetic value independent of their resemblance to natural objects. For example, the painter may speak solely through linear design and pure color, through skillful arrangement of his basic materials. This is not to say that the argument must be followed to its logical conclusion, refusal to allow any natural likeness whatever to clutter a picture. Fry was careful to point out that the degree of representation depends upon the subject at hand; if the artist wishes to show a tiger attacking a man, the animal should look like a tiger, but if he wishes to convey the

[4] "Post-Impressionism," *The Fortnightly Review*, Vol. LXXXIX, No. dxxxiii (May 1, 1911), 856–67.

idea of an animal's attack upon a man, all that matters is that the composition express ferocity and savagery.

Fry intended that the term Post-Impressionism designate a tendency rather than a closely knit school. It had both a chronological and an aesthetic significance. The Post-Impressionist rejected the doctrine of his immediate predecessors, and he did so because it seemed to him the inevitable but final development of the representational standards accepted during the Renaissance and succeeding centuries. The Impressionist had emphasized accidental patterns of light and color which everyday perception neglects for other, more practical matters, and had produced work which did not necessarily resemble a subject as it presents itself to the ordinary spectator. Concentrating only upon certain aspects of a scene, he tended to break up its unity, and he was therefore given credit for producing a new art. Actually, his art was still representational; it was merely representation of an extraordinary kind of perception, and the Post-Impressionist wished to avoid this approach.

A step toward a purely abstract art, Post-Impressionism attracted such English painters as Wyndham Lewis, who exhibited some of his early work at the Grafton show. It appealed to those who felt that aesthetic judgment should be freed from its bias in favor of representation and to those who were convinced that the technical problems of painting needed more attention. It sought to divert spectator judgment from verisimilitude to matters of form or arrangement, volume or dimension. It placed the responsibility for creation squarely upon the artist himself.

Another attack upon tradition was made by F. T. Marinetti and the Futurists, who announced a program for poetry as well as for painting. Futurist doctrine was an explosive mixture of aesthetics and social propaganda, and, though it concentrated upon literary and artistic aims, its implications appear in retrospect to have been most strongly social. Nor were Marinetti and his disciples particularly subtle in their effort to disguise the nonaesthetic aspects of their doctrine. They advocated "semi-equality of man and woman, diminution of the difference between their social rights" and hoped that sexual equality and consequent freedom for the female would destroy the enervating concept of love.[5] Assuming a "complete renewal of human sensibility which has taken place since the great scientific discoveries," they glorified the values of the modern consciousness. They made a fetish of speed and praised the quickened tempo of twentieth-century life; they deprecated quiet living as inappropriate to a machine age and substituted love of danger and a surrender to the vital impulses as their guiding principles; they loosed a bolt at established religion by recommending that modern man concern himself less with the *beyond* and more with the events of his exciting worldly existence; they voiced a horror of all features of the past and looked to newness as their standard of value.

The Futurist's poetic theory was suitably extreme. His poems were primarily lyrical, expressing the feelings consequent upon realization of the intoxicating glories of modern life. Since these emotions are stifled by the commonly accepted rules of syntax and punctuation, they must be set free; hence Marinetti's "words at liberty," for which he paradoxically claimed "a mathematical order and [a] geometrical splendour." He argued that when one wishes to

[5] F. T. Marinetti, "Wireless Imagination and Words at Liberty," trans. by Arundel del Re, *Poetry and Drama*, Vol. I, No. 3 (September, 1913), 319–26.

express lyric feelings, he finds it necessary to "chuck adjectives and punctuation overboard," to spread, to broadcast, "handfuls of essential words." "Words at liberty" were to be supplemented by the "Wireless imagination":

an entire freedom of images and analogies expressed by disjointed words and without the connecting wires of syntax. Images [are] the very life-blood of poetry. Poetry must be an uninterrupted sequence of new images.

Marinetti laid down specific rules for the technique of the wireless imagination and words at liberty. He urged the poet

1. To divest the substantive of adjectives. "We tend everywhere toward suppressing the qualifying adjective, because it presupposes an interruption in intuition, a too minute definition of the substantive." While he permitted occasional use of the adjective to give atmosphere, or tone, or to regulate the speed of analogies, he insisted that it be plainly separated from words at liberty by brackets or a perpendicular line.

2. To abolish the different moods and tenses of the verb, except where needed to convey essential contrasts or to effect changes in rhythm.

3. To establish the infinitive as the basic tense of the verb, because it "IS THE MOTION OF THE NEW LYRICISM, having from time to time the value and rapidity of a train wheel, the screw of an aeroplane or of a Gnôme monoplane." By its mood it keeps words from "sitting down in sentences," it is essential to "violent and dynamic lyrical expression."

4. To employ mathematical signs instead of standard punctua-

tion. ✕, +, =, and > indicate more directly the movements the reader's mind is supposed to take.

5. To develop precision and brevity and avoid vague connotations. Not: "a vast and deep chime"; but: "belchime extension 20 kmg."

6. To introduce numbers "intuitively."

7. To use "Free and Expressive" typography and orthography. In this way one can convey "FACIAL MIMICRY AND THE GESTICULATIONS OF THE NARRATOR." The writer may ask for three or four different colors of ink and twenty different forms of type in the same article; he may even augment or diminish the number of vowels and consonants in words.[6]

One principle deserves special consideration. "Our love of matter, our will to penetrate it, to feel its vibrations and the physical sympathy that binds us to engines, incite us to use onomatopoeia."[7] Marinetti and the Futurists worked out an elaborate analysis and classification of onomatopoeic effects obtainable in poetry. The "Direct imitative elementary realistic" onomatopoeia keeps expression from becoming too abstract by introducing into poetry the sounds of the natural or man-made world. Marinetti's argument for the practical value of this device:

The strident onomatopoeia *ssiiiiii* renders the whistle of a tug on the Mose, and is followed by the veiled onomatopoeia *ffiiiii*

[6] *Ibid.;* "A Futurist Manifesto," trans. by Arundel del Re, *The New Age*, Vol. XV, No. 1 (May 7, 1914), 16–17.

[7] "Abstract Onomatopoeia and Numeric Sensibility," *The New Age*, Vol. XV, No. 11 (July 16, 1914), 255.

fiiiiii echoing from the other shore. The two onomatopoeias have saved my having to describe the width of the river.

A second type is the "Indirect Complex and Analogical Onomatopoeia"; *dum-dum-dum,* for example, represents the "rotative noise" of the African sun and the orange color of the sky, "thereby creating a relationship between sensations of weight, heat, colour, smell and noise." Third, the Futurist cited the "abstract" type, "which expresses a mental state" and does not imitate audible sounds; in conclusion, he pointed to the "Psycho-onomatopoeic Chord," which is a fusion of two or three abstract onomatopoeias.

The application of these principles is poetic anarchy.

Battle
Weight $+$ Smell

Sun gold billets dishes lead sky silk heat bedquilting purple blue torrefaction Sun=volcano+3000 flags atmosphere precision corrida fury surgeon lamp rays history sparks linen desert clinic×20000 arms 2000 feet 10000 eyesights scintillations expectation operation sand ship-engines Italian Arabs.

"Battle" typifies words at liberty; its expression is in no way hindered by the wires of syntax or by punctuation; though it fails to designate its adjectives, the failure is perhaps the translator's, and, in any case, it uses them sparingly and achieves its effect by a catalogue of substantives, "synthesized" in certain places by mathematical signs and punctuated in others by "intuitive" numbers. Individual images are presented clearly, but the total picture is broken, and "one naturally arrives at a multiform emotional perspective."

Against this verse should be placed a less extreme Futurist experiment.

Oh the Earth, and its symmetry, and the curves of its
  geometry
and its walk of a lazy donkey
which, blindfold, drives in a circle
the flaring wheel of the sun; and it draws for evermore,
adulterated light out of the depth of space. . . .
Oh the Earth! . . . Oh the Earth? . . . Alas, the nausea
  of living
crouched on its shoulders: we are like performing monkeys
frilled and adorned and brought to the fair. . . .

The poet has observed none of Futurism's more striking rules; neither his syntax, punctuation, spelling, or typography is notably unorthodox. Instead, the poem looks for its effect to the originality of the two principal metaphors, one (lines 2–4) whose statement is somewhat unsound as science but acceptable as poetry, another (lines 6–8) whose comparison just escapes banality by apt selection of the characteristics upon which it is based.

The Imagists were interested in Futurism, but kept their distance. Flint devoted one of his *Poetry and Drama* "French Chronicles" to a discussion of the movement's activity in France. In 1914, Aldington described it as "the most powerful artistic force" of the day, his interpretation suggesting that its objective rules attracted less notice than certain more obvious surface characteristics. "Futurism, as I see it, is a state of mind. It implies that one lives in the great center of Anglo-Saxon civilisation, and that one acts and thinks and writes accordingly."[8] While the transition

[8] "Reviews," *The Egoist*, Vol. I, No. 13 (July 1, 1914), 247.

from Futurism to nationalism was reasonable enough, he
refused to face the literal meaning of the Futurist shout,
"destroy museums, libraries"; he chose, instead, to believe
that since modern art is not cut off from the past, Futurist
glorification of the modern did not mean rejection of all
work produced before the turn of the century. Lawrence
shared Aldington's admiration, but expressed a definite and
important reservation:

> I have been interested in the futurists. . . . I like [Futurism]
> because it is the applying to emotions the purging of old forms
> and sentimentalities. I like it for its saying—enough of this sickly
> cant, let us be honest and stick by what is in us. . . . They want
> to deny every scrap of tradition and experience, which is silly. . . .
> I like them. Only I don't believe in them.[9]

Pound attended Futurist meetings and even occupied a seat
on the platform reserved for the speaker and the more distinguished members of the audience, but he soon realized
what the doctrine implied and took his stand against it. He
wrote in *Poetry:* "There is nothing like futurist abolition
of past glories in this brief article."[10] Following the Vorticist
party line, he condemned Futurism as "accelerated impressionism," as encouraging formless glorification of the individual's reactions to the modern world.

Yet Imagism and Futurism shared a surprising number
of beliefs. Both rigidly restricted the use of the adjective,
as merely impeding the communicative efficiency of the substantive. Both proclaimed the need of the modern poet for
a free form of verse. Both condemned rhetoric. Both (the

[9] *Letters,* 197–98.
[10] "The Renaissance," *Poetry,* Vol. V, No. 5 (February, 1915), 230.

Futurist more aggressively than the Imagist) asserted the importance of complete freedom for the play of images and analogies. Futurism's vigor and energy, its hatred of the stylized, sentimental, and academic, and its concentration on its own times had an undeniable appeal to the Imagism of the early years.

The Futurist program for the painter likewise attracted considerable temporary notice. Marinetti proclaimed the artist's duty to turn his attention toward the subjects peculiarly associated with a mechanized society:

> There is born to-day a new beauty which I shall call GEO-METRIC and MECHANICAL SPLENDOUR. . . .
> Nothing is more beautiful than a great central power station, that contains the hydraulic pressure of a chain of mountains and the electric force of a vast horizon synthesized in the marble distributing slabs, bristling with meters and levers and shining commutators.[11]

Marinetti and Nevinson, the latter the principal Futurist artist in England, printed a manifesto which they sent to the leading newspapers and showered on people in the stalls and dress circles of the theaters. Their creed shared certain general aims with that of the poet, opposing worship of tradition, excoriating the effeminacy and the purely decorative nature of English art, and advocating a more virile, anti-sentimental attitude and an advance guard of artists who would not stand in fear of the "Academes."

The painting done in accordance with Futurist principles theoretically, and sometimes actually, used line, color,

[11] "A Futurist Manifesto," *The New Age*, Vol. XV, No. 1 (May 7, 1914), 16.

form to communicate a sense of the flux and vitality of life. Giacomo Balla's *Leash in Motion*, for example, conveys a feeling for movement by including, in one image, various positions assumed by a leash as a dog to which it is attached steps along at a brisk rate (the dog's motions are recorded, too, as well as those of the feet of the person walking it). Balla is interested less in the objective scene than in the quality that can be felt in it, here a quality to which the Futurist felt the modern should be especially receptive. The Futurist insisted that "no picture should be a mere representation"; his works were to be judged not according to their resemblance to what the untrained eye sees, but according to the effectiveness with which they reproduced the impression. However, his emphasis was upon subject matter rather than form, which he did not study as in itself capable of evoking an aesthetic experience. While the composition as a whole did not represent an ordinary preception (the feeling he sought to convey was often too complex to be communicated by any of the traditional techniques), the Futurist was none the less dealing with natural materials; he was still reflecting nature, though his more extreme work was likely to confound the uninitiated.

The immediate stimulus to the formation of Vorticism was Wyndham Lewis's opposition to Marinetti. Futurism had seemed exciting and valuable, but its preoccupation with man and his machines alienated many English artists. Lewis objected not merely to its relationship to Impressionism but to its

Automobilism and Nietzsche stunt.

With a lot of good sense and vitality at his disposal, he hammers away in the blatant mechanism of his manifestoes, at his *idée fixé* of Modernity. . . .

He snarls and bawls about the Past and Future with all his Italian practical directness.

This is of great use when one considers with what sort of person the artist today has to deal! . . .

Cannot Marinetti, sensible and energetic man that he is, be induced to throw over this sentimental rubbish about Automobiles and Aeroplanes, and follow his friend Balla into a purer religion of art?[12]

This was essentially the reaction of Henri Gaudier-Brzeska and of Pound. Gaudier referred to Futurist emotions as "of a superficial character, verging on the vulgar," and Pound stated flatly: "I am wholly opposed to his [Marinetti's] principles."[13]

These three, under Lewis's guidance, organized Vorticism as a countermovement. Since both Post-Impressionism and Futurism were importations, they tried to give their movement a nationalistic appeal, proclaiming that "the modern world is due almost entirely to Anglo-Saxon genius" and that the English above all other nations should be receptive to the new art inherent in modern life: "They are the inventors of this bareness and hardness, and should be the great enemies of Romance."[14] The strain of national pride seemed the only difference between the Vorticists and the followers of Marinetti. Violet Hunt recalls that Lewis "was hard put to it to describe the neat distinction between the

[12] "The Melodrama of Modernity," *Blast*, Vol. I, No. 1 (June 20, 1914), 143–44.

[13] "The Allied Artists Association, Ltd.," *The Egoist*, Vol. I, No. 6 (March 16, 1914); "Vorticism," *The Fortnightly Review*, Vol. LXXXIX, No. dxxxiii (May 1, 1911), 468.

[14] "Manifesto," *Blast*, Vol. I, No. 1 (June 20, 1914), 39, 41.

two schools. The simplest image, says he, is to take that of the vortex. 'You think at once of a whirlpool. At the heart of the whirlpool is a great silent place where all the energy is concentrated. And there, at the point of concentration is the Vorticist.' "[15] That is not particularly concise, and one feels that Vorticism's attempt to startle the Englishman into awareness of his responsibility to modern art may merely have substituted English for Italian noise. Through *Blast*, whose aggressive tone shocked many readers and obscured whatever serious intent the movement might have had, Vorticism brought its ideas to the attention of the public. *Blast* avowedly aimed to shock, to "make the rich of the community shed their education skin, to destroy politeness, standardization and academicism," and it was so successful that its extremism and rudeness were about all its public noticed.

Yet, despite its garish manner, Vorticism advocated serious doctrine. Probably its most insistent and assertive theme was the need for greater vigor and energy in the arts. Here it was in direct competition with Marinetti; as John Cournos has expressed it, "*energy* was the great cry of both schools" even though "one energy is 'dispersed' and the other 'stationary.' "[16] The Vorticist, however, stood firm against any move to reject either the past or the present for the future.

Our vortex is not afraid of the Past: it
    has forgotten its existence.
Our vortex regards the Future as as sentimental
    as the Past.

[15] *I Have This to Say* (New York, 1926), 211.
[16] "The Death of Futurism," *The Egoist*, Vol. IV, No. 1 (January, 1917), 6.

The new vortex plunges to the heart of the Present. . . .
The Vorticist is at his maximum point of energy
  when stillest.[17]

Further, it insisted upon the weakness of art which relies
for its appeal upon natural scenes and objects, thus linking
its attitude with that of the Post-Impressionists and looking
toward a purely abstract art.

Intrinsic beauty is in the Interpreter and Seer,
  not in the object or content.
We do not want to change the appearance
  of the world, because we are not
  Naturalists, Impressionists, or Futurists . . . ,
  and do not depend on the appearance of the
  world for our art.

Through the writing of individual members, there runs
another theme: the belief in the abstract as the only approach
which can restore intellectual strength to modern art. Lewis,
like Roger Fry in his explanation of Post-Impressionism,
attacked Impressionism as merely a development of century-
old standards which judged art according to how closely it
approximated nature; calling for new standards which
would measure value in terms of the artist's imaginative
exploration of his material, he dismissed nature as of no
significance. Reality exists not in life, but in the artist's ability to organize, to create a pattern from the material given
him by life. Particularly, the Vorticist was attracted to those
forms characteristic of the modern age, the geometric figures, planes, cubes, the rigid lines of the machine, but not,
like the Futurist, to the machine itself.

[17] "Our Vortex," *Blast*, Vol. I, No. 1 (June 20, 1914), 147-48.

Gaudier argued in a similar vein for the sculptor.

The acceptable doctrine of my generation is
  Sculptural feeling is the appreciation of
    masses in relation.
  Sculptural ability is the defining of
    these masses by planes.

I SHALL DERIVE MY EMOTIONS SOLELY FROM THE *ARRANGEMENT OF SURFACES*. I shall present my emotions by the ARRANGEMENT OF MY SUR-FACES, THE PLANES AND LINES BY WHICH THEY ARE DEFINED.[18]

He was known especially for his attacks upon the art of "those *damn* Greeks," whom he condemned as totally lack-ing in the sense of form. Their art copied the natural, and was therefore derivative; they "petrified" their own "sem-blance." Although he later tempered his enthusiasm for the abstract in sculpture, his Vorticist affiliation expressed a sin-cere antagonism toward the standard which allows an artist to rely upon pleasure at the sight of the human form rather than his own skillful use of material.

Pound's comments upon art indicate a taste similar to that of Lewis and Gaudier. It was mainly Vorticism's exclu-sive emphasis upon the formal elements as expressive of a concentrated energy that attracted him. He has said that as early as 1911 he had become interested in a nonrepresenta-tional art, one that "would speak only by arrangements in

[18] Quoted by Pound, "Affirmations," *The New Age*, Vol. XVI, No. 14 (February 4, 1915), 382; *Gaudier-Brzeska: A Memoir* (London and New York, 1916), 20, 116.

colour," and had even considered founding a school devoted to this principal. He also acknowledged a debt to Jacob Epstein and, grudgingly, to Hulme.

So far as I am concerned, Jacob Epstein was the first person who came talking about "form, not the *form of anything*." It may have been Mr. T. E. Hulme, quoting Epstein. I don't know that it matters much who said it first; he may have been a theorist with no more than a sort of scientific gift for discovery. He may have been a great sculptor capable of acting out his belief.[19]

In any case, the briefs of Hulme, Lewis, Epstein, and others for the abstract found him a sympathetic listener, and encouraged him to add his voice to theirs.

Pleasure is derivable not only from the stroking or pushing of the retina by light waves of various colour, BUT ALSO by the impact of these waves in certain arranged tracts.

This simple and obvious fact is the basis of the "modern" "art" "revolution."

The eye *likes* certain plainnesses, certain complexities, certain varieties, certain incitements, certain reliefs and suspensions.

It likes these things irrespective of whether or no they form a replica of known objects.[20]

As usual, he drew an analogy with music, which is in the same way an "expression by means of an arrangement of

19 "Affirmations," *The New Age*, Vol. XVI, No. 3 (February 4, 1915), 350.
20 *Pavannes and Divisions*, 255.

sound," and even traced the origin of Vorticism to Pater's statement: "All arts approach the conditions of music."[21] He not only became an enthusiastic Vorticist but attempted to make the doctrine applicable to poetry. A month before he was discarded by the Imagists he had converted his Imagism into Vorticism, and when Vorticism was announced, the manifesto embraced Imagism in its somewhat rude grasp: "The English Parallel Movement to Cubism and Expressionism. Imagism in Poetry. Death-blow to Impressionism and Futurism and all the Refuse of Naïf Science."

The bond between Imagism and Vorticism, between the image in poetry and the abstract in art, is not immediately apparent. Pound's theory of the primary pigment which links all the arts is not, at face value, a satisfactory explanation. If true, it would certainly establish the image as the formal element which is peculiarly the property of the poet, and it would place the imagist poet with the abstract artist among the *avant-garde*. But, as Pound had to admit in connection with his "Metro" poem, the image involved color and might better have found expression in painting. An image is often effective just because it involves qualities of the plastic, of line and color, which properly are the primary pigments of some other art.

What, then, was the bond between Vorticism and Imagism? The only reasonable answer is suggested in two statements by Pound, who, on these occasions, was not specifically attempting to justify the relationship.

Art comes from intellect stirred by will, impulse, emotion; but art is emphatically not any of these others deprived of intellect,

---

[21] Pound also included his definition of the Image as forming another branch of the ancestry of Vorticism.

and out drunk on its 'lone, saying that it is "that which is beyond the intelligence."

The test of invention lies in the primary pigment, that is to say, in that part of any art which is peculiarly of that art as distinct from "the other arts." The vorticist maintains that the organizing or creative-inventive faculty is the thing that matters.[22]

Art is a product of two forces. It is a product of energy or emotion; here he was in agreement with both the Vorticist and the Futurist—in revolt against the lack of strength in the derivative art of his time. It is also a product of the artist's inventiveness, the original and vigorous application of intellect to subject matter; here he parted company with the Futurist, who emphasized formlessness as a means to unrestricted self-expression. Both Pound's Imagism and Vorticism insisted that art be, in his own words, an *equation* for the emotion and not the emotion itself. Both felt that this effort to objectify emotions was the element needed in modern art, and Pound associated most closely with the new painting and the new sculpture those of his poems which, like "Heather," he could describe as "objective realities." "Heather" is simply an exercise in the creation of an effective pattern of color images, the sleek black and the delicate but brilliant orange of the first stanza contrasting sharply with the rich white and glossy green of the second. The effect depends solely upon this contrast in color; whatever pleasure the poem may give has its source here, and the objects used as vehicles for the colors matter hardly at all, except as by their connotations they contribute to the texture of the colors used.

[22] "Affirmations," *The New Age*, Vol. XVI, No. 14 (February 4, 1915), 381; *ibid.*, Vol. XVI, No. 13 (January 28, 1915), 349–50.

An even better illustration appears in another of the poems of the *Lustra* volume, poems written during or just after his Vorticist period. "A Song of the Degrees" works from the same principle of arrangement of colors, and, as it is a slightly longer poem, reveals more convincingly its dependence upon purely formal and structural qualities. Stanza I establishes the "theme" the poem will develop, a contrast between restful Chinese colors and the artificial, evil colors refracted through the glass of an object before the poet, as it were a still life, from which certain colors are abstracted and heightened in significance by juxtaposition with others from the poet's memory. The reader, as the poem progresses, feels only the rigidly controlled, opposing responses to the natural silver and gold of wheat, sun, and bright stone (stanza II) and to the forced or "made" hues of amber and gold filtered in two-faced iridescence through the prism (stanza III). "A Song of the Degrees" is dehumanized in the sense approved by the abstractionist; only the "Why am I warned? Why am I sent away?" of stanza III seem to disturb the poem's abstract, objective reality, inviting curiosity about the poet rather than about the structure of his poem, but, except at this debatable point, the poem has no "content" in the conventional sense of the term. Its only content is its form or structure, and it is so consistently objective that it *is* a reality in itself, the poet having withdrawn from view entirely. It is a Vortex or Image.

As they are objective, "inventive," as they force the artist to creation of a form that is organic and that must make its appeal strictly on the basis of its organic nature and not on that of irrelevant matters of content, Imagist poetry and Vorticist painting are related, are modern, and are in the way one feels Pound intended, hard; they may be said to employ the primary pigment of any art. These poems also employ the image, which he had called the primary pigment of poetry because it involves the fresh, clear, colorful natural detail and the psychological impact that accompanies the word or phrase standing for this detail—in both a literal and a psychological or aesthetic sense it is what gives poetry its coloring. Emotion or energy gives the image, by which he said he did not mean the explanatory metaphor, though he admitted the exact border line was difficult to draw; but, more important, the images are so arranged that the pattern becomes an Image, an organic structure giving a force and a pleasure that are greater than and different from the images alone. Pound had criticized the Imagists for the looseness of their poetry, which employed the image without the sense of form that would transform imagery into the Image; Vorticism was a means of reinforcing this criticism.

Hulme's relation to this pattern is of some interest, and little has been said so far about the portion of his aesthetic that bore upon the visual rather than the linguistic arts. If his poetic theory was predicated upon a refusal to grant intuition the power to comprehend reality and approximated the view of "Cinders," his theories about painting and sculpture conceded a limited authority to intuition and thus approached the philosophy of "Humanism and the Religious Attitude." It would be convenient to describe the pessimism of "Cinders" as his original position and the concessions of "Humanism" as a revised and therefore later view, but Herbert Read's statement that the "Cinders" are notes entered up to 1917 makes it unwise to assert such a development too confidently. Nevertheless, the dates of published articles and Hulme's own account of his growing interest in art strongly support it. He had published articles discussing aspects of philosophy as early as 1908 and in this and the next two years had given considerable attention to his poetry clubs; not until 1912–14 (approximately the date of his first public statements on humanism and the religious attitude) does he begin to express an interest in modern art.

According to his account, the trend began when he rejected the philosophy of the Renaissance. Presumably he was referring to his conviction of the necessity for a philosophy of intuition as opposed to the mechanistic, humanistic philosophies which originated in Renaissance thought and were given their fullest development by the nineteenth century. He apparently felt that his discontinuity theory provided the first and fundamental link between his attitude and that underlying modern art. However, he did not realize the relationship until, studying examples of pre-Renaissance (Byzantine) mosaic, he recognized that their geometrical basis was the suitable expression of the religious attitude and paralleled the efforts of his friends among contemporary artists.

For specific theory he was indebted to the German writer Wilhelm Worringer, whom he discovered to have views similar to his own and with whom he discussed the matter in the course of a visit to Berlin. Worringer's *Form Problems of the Gothic* attacked the tendency to regard the art of Classical antiquity as the only appropriate standard for aesthetic judgment and attempted to place the Classical in a historical perspective which would reduce its position to a significance more in conformity to the facts of cultural history. He recognized three principal types of art and traced each to a set of basic attitudes towards the universe. His *primitive man*, fearing the forces of a universe he was not equipped to comprehend and in his art emphasizing lifeless geometric forms which seemed to offer the stability he sought, and his *oriental man*, better able to identify the divine, accepting a dualistic universe as his sublime fate, and in his art, through the expressionless line and surface, conveying a concept of an order higher than his own, merge into Hulme's *classical man*. Worringer's *classical man*, representative of classical antiquity, feeling himself master of his world, establishing himself as the measure of all things, and in his art glorifying the natural line, corresponds to Hulme's *romantic man*.

According to Hulme, romantic art was meant to produce in the spectator a heightened feeling of vitality. It represents a liking for the forms and movements found in nature because the natural is considered as reflecting the divine. It is representative art in the sense that the objects depicted resemble the actual objects they represent; the artist aims to capture as closely as possible the natural appearance of his material. Geometric art, on the other hand, rises from a feeling of separation between man and nature and from the satisfaction of imposing some constant and absolute form upon an unruly universe. It tends to the abstract forms of geometry as representative of a perfection which nature can never achieve and thus is consistent with Hulme's religious or classical attitude.

The theory permits two objections, one of which Hulme ignored and one of which he tried to answer. Abstract forms are apparently meant to symbolize reality or the absolute, if not to fulfill the requirements of direct communication. They stand in his aesthetic in the same relation to the realm of the human or vital as *perfection* and *virtue* stood in his philosophy as a whole. In both cases he has identified absolute values with abstraction. One feels that Hulme's at-

tempt to be specific may reveal an inconsistency in his thinking. Although Hulme insisted that the values of religion
and ethics differed absolutely from those of the vital or intellectual, abstractions would seem to be only products of
the intellect. He did not touch upon the problem either because he did not see it as a problem or because he did not
see it at all.

He recognized the second objection and discussed it
without proposing a complete answer. One value of pure
form, according to his thought, was its antivital nature, its
lack of vitality: it reflects the divine because it is the anti-
thesis of the vital. In this sense he was perhaps justified in
establishing abstraction, a product of intellect, as symbolic
of the divine which intellect cannot know. But he hoped at
the same time to justify the appeal of pure form to normal,
human emotions.

If form has no dramatic or human aesthetic interest, then it is
obviously stupid for a human to be interested in it. . . . I think it
could be shown that the emotions produced by abstract form, are
the ordinary everyday human emotions—they are produced in
a different way, that is all.[23]

He argued that our consciousness of an interest in form
proves its effect upon some human emotion within us. The
feeling is probably that of pleasure at skillful arrangement
of material; but whether this is an intellectual or an emotional satisfaction and whether it can, in either case, lead to
an intuition of the antivital are questions which Hulme fails
to discuss.

[23] "Modern Art," *The New Age*, Vol. XV, No. 10 (July 9, 1914),
231.

It is clear, however, that he considered pure form and such abstractions as *perfection* and *virtue* in some way related to the absolutes of religion and ethics, and his theory of art was meant to be consistent with this belief. Art was conceded the power to reveal glimpses of a reality beyond man which he had not granted to poetry. In fact, he cited the interests of contemporary art as a hopeful sign that the humanist tradition might be weakening.

May not the change of sensibility, in a region like aesthetics, a by-path in which we are, as it were, off our guard, be some indication that the *humanist tradition is breaking up*—for individuals here and there, at any rate?[24]

Hulme watched the Vorticists closely, but he would not join them officially and was eventually satisfied by Vorticist behavior that his caution had been wise. It is apparent, however, that he and the Vorticist shared two important beliefs: they rejected the classical and Renaissance limitation of aesthetic feeling to the pleasure derivable from contemplation of the human and natural; and they substituted a criterion which forced the artist to rely for his effects upon perception and manipulation of form. Although Hulme had worked out a reasoned justification of these beliefs and the Vorticists had not, their manifestoes offer some evidence of a basic philosophical attitude similar to his. Hulme accepted only the aspects of Bergson's thought which proved the limitation of man's intellect and ignored those which dealt with the *élan vital* and implied a glorification and intensification of the irrational impulse; the Vorticist rejected Bergson categorically and included him in a list of persons and

24 *Speculations*, 53.

qualities to be "blasted." Lewis called him "the philosopher of Impressionism," authority for the weak and dangerous aesthetic which looks upon Nature as synonymous with richness and freshness, which talks of "LIFE . . . instead of ART."

For similar reasons, Hulme and the Vorticists attacked Futurism: it praised the irrational; constructed its aesthetic upon a bacchanalian acceptance of LIFE; and advocated an art whose formlessness, meant to allow completely free expression of individual feeling, was exactly the quality the abstract artist hoped to correct. Marinetti was a gregarious, machine-age Rousseau, preaching a romanticism which called for the release of the emotions and intensification of life, but accepting the works of modern society instead of rejecting them. Hulme and the Vorticist were antiromantic, concerned with deprecating the significance of the individual and his "inspiration," with encouraging a more serious study of the technical aspects of art—which were, however, to define, express, the material of a feeling as vigorous as that which the Futurist glorified.

This interest in form, in a complete objectification, is what characterizes the "new" developments in art. Impressionism and Futurism were, according to the moderns, descendent from the anti-intellectual, vital, anthropocentric standards of romanticism, however experimental they seemed to be in their approach. Post-Impressionism and Vorticism (in its earnest moments) were new and modern in their effort to check the further growth of these ideals by shifting the emphasis to the intellectual and antivital, to the subordination of life to art, to an attitude which closely parallels Hulme's classicism. Symbolism, as we have seen, subscribed to both sets of values: it had a romantic theoretical background, but in actual practice its poetry revealed a meticulous formalism, submerging personality in the form of expression, with which the moderns could sympathize.

The new emphasis is implicit in Imagism, which was also fundamentally opposed to Futurism: the Futurist sublimated the vital feelings, giving them the authority of cosmic forces; the Imagist sought to avoid the cosmic. The Futurist wanted a free expression of individual feeling; the Imagist asserted the insignificance of the personal reaction as such. Hulme's poetic theory condemned romantic intuition and centered attention on the poet's ability to draw new analogies from the world around him; the measure of the poet's success was determined almost entirely by the effect of his newly revealed comparisons. H. D.'s poetry is certainly personal and distinctive in its tone; but her early poems just as certainly limit the feelings so rigidly to the concrete that personality has relatively little meaning here. Her poetry is a means of bringing content under careful, efficient control instead of allowing it to overflow onto the page. Her technique, as well as Hulme's and Pound's, demands intellectual effort from the writer by insisting upon selection of the most expressive image, and so far as "Amygism" ignored this aspect of the doctrine its significance as a "new" development is diminished.

Finally, when Pound published the principles of Imagism in 1913, a year before he became associated with Vorticism, he did not mention subject matter; the principles were all technical, having to do with the form of expression rather than content. And the same may be said generally of the manifestoes published in the anthologies of 1915 and 1916. Perhaps the interest in the nonrepresentational was an admission that the artist really had little of significance to say; perhaps the "dehumanization" of art was, as some insist, a token of defeat. But the new concerns at least provided some excuse for a re-examination of the fundamentals of expression, and this, in turn, gave them some excuse, which they could not find in their "message," for continuing to write and paint, for continuing to exist as artists; that they were not looking simply for the new is indicated by their rejection of Futurism. It is to this tradition that Imagism clearly belongs, giving to modern poetry its experimental direction; in this general pattern of aesthetic theory Imagism has its fullest meaning (though of the Imagists, only Pound immediately saw his school in this perspective): as one manifestation of the new century's realization of the need to make form once again meaningful and expressive.

IX

Conclusion

I F ONE DEFINED the technique in terms of Hulme's
clever manipulation of simple analogies or in terms
of the clear, sharp, essentially surface and descriptive
imagery of "Oread" or Pound's "Metro" poem, the
limitations of Imagism were clear enough. Hulme's theory
was open to the objection that it would make poetry an
amusing game, even if a somewhat difficult one. Pound's
theory seemed to permit charges equally as damaging: it
would restrict poetry to the single image, make the long
poem an impossibility, and refuse to admit the importance
of ideas or "meaning" in verse, though these restrictions
were implicit in his illustrations of Imagism rather than
explicit in his manifesto, and disappear upon more careful
examination of his practice and his poetic criticism. While
not fully justified, these interpretations also suggested a
failure of attention to the structure of a poem—to the idea
of a poem as structure.

There was, within the movement, a considerable amount
of resistance to the doctrine. Lawrence, of course, was not
close enough to the members of the school to be much concerned with its aims, but Flint had his own ideas about
poetry and Fletcher was often in open rebellion against

even the loose and general principles of the prefaces. Aldington and Amy Lowell wrote some lines that fall within the theory, strictly interpreted, but only H. D. wrote consistently the kind of verse that Pound at first demanded of the Imagists, and neither she nor Pound confined themselves to this early idea. Verse that approximates Hulme's is a rarity. At its best, Imagism was only a phase in the artistic development of a small group of writers, though its effects remain apparent in their later work.

The limitations were just as well understood outside the immediate Imagist circle, and it is not surprising that Imagist poetry can claim few writers wholly devoted to its principles. Failing to exact full support from its own members, and never, except in the little-known theory of Hulme, clearly defined, it could hardly have encouraged unquestioning support from others. Its doctrine was, however, of interest to one important poet whose association with the group has already been described; and although Pound carefully explained that his discovery, T. S. Eliot, was no Imagist and although Eliot at no time advocated the program, certain of his poems seem to reflect his close acquaintance with the movement's theory and practice.

Early published articles show that, even more fully than Pound, he understood the nature and function of the image in verse. Of Mina Loy, he wrote: "she needs the support of the image, even if only as the instant point of departure; in this poem she becomes abstract, and the word separates from the thing."[1] Nor did he allow *image* to acquire a convenient ambiguity; it is the device by which the poet brings the reader into direct contact with his subject,

[1] "Observations," *The Egoist*, Vol. V, No. 5 (May, 1918), 70. Signed "T. S. Apteryx."

and, as such, involves comparison and analogy. Eliot's views admittedly and approvingly paraphrased De Gourmont:

all thought and all language is based ultimately upon a few simple physical movements. Metaphor is not something applied externally for the adornment of style, it is the life of style, of language. The healthy metaphor adds to the strength of the language; it makes available some of that physical source of energy upon which the life of language depends.[2]

Like Hulme, like Hueffer and the Imagists, he believed that one of the principal efforts of contemporary poetry should be "to recover the accents of direct speech."[3] He did not offer this simply as a statement about diction, but as a comment on the whole question of subject matter and the poet's attitude toward it. If the poet chooses to deal with the cosmic, his language will naturally reflect the choice; but if he chooses to deal with the external object, he will tend less toward the literary and the rhetorical. It is difficult to write bombastically about the smell of steaks in passageways or about the moon if it reminds you of a red-faced farmer.

Eliot distinguished two ways in which the problem of subject, attitude, and diction had been solved by his contemporaries. The American solution was "to arrest at the object" without relating it to any emotion. This, of course, often results in a superficial, descriptive objectivity; it was Amy Lowell's *externality*, explained more succinctly than she had been able to explain it. The English poets, on the

[2] "Studies in Contemporary Criticism," *The Egoist*, Vol. V, No. 9 (October, 1918), 114.
[3] "Reflections on Contemporary Poetry," *The Egoist*, Vol. IV, No. 8 (September 1, 1917), 118.

other hand, solved the problem by concentrating their attention upon the trivial, accidental, or commonplace, the result being an unliterary, conversational idiom. No verse better illustrates this carefully calculated introduction of the trivial and commonplace than that of Eliot, and of Hulme.

After "Portrait of a Lady" (1909) and "The Love Song of J. Alfred Prufrock" (1910), both dramatic monologues, Eliot wrote two poems, "Preludes" and "Rhapsody on a Windy Night," which in many ways satisfy the requirements of Imagism. Written after his arrival in England, they are concerned with personal feelings, conveying a reaction to scenes of modern city life, offering no hint of transcendental implications. The "Preludes" especially are reminiscent of one aspect of Imagism: they treat their subjects directly by depending upon the image to communicate meaning to the reader; their impact is explained by the imagery which the reader sees, feels, or even smells for himself.

> *The winter evening settles down*
> *With smell of steaks in passageways.*
> *Six o'clock.*
> *The burnt-out ends of smoky days.*
> *And now a gusty shower wraps*
> *The grimy scraps*
> *Of withered leaves about your feet*
> *And newspapers from vacant lots;*
> *The showers beat*
> *On broken blinds and chimney-pots,*
> *And at the corner of the street*
> *A lonely cab-horse steams and stamps.*
> *And then the lighting of the lamps.*

The tone of the poem is established by the succession of images, and, like much Imagist verse, this is descriptive; but the selection of images is so careful and so representative that they assume a limited symbolic range—they become analytical rather than merely descriptive, or, to use Pound's phraseology, they evoke rather than describe; but they evoke a human, individual feeling or state of mind, and their range is limited to this. The one metaphor contained in the lines quoted translates the abstract into terms of the concrete, the poetic (days) into the decidedly mundane and commonplace (burnt-out cigar or cigarette ends).

One function of the metaphors, then, is to produce an effect of shock upon recognition of relationships newly perceived, with an additional touch of irony deriving from the nature of the relationship established.

Unlike the Imagists, who owed Hulme only a sense of the importance of the image, Eliot was at this time writing a verse whose closest parallels are with the theory of Hulme. He had begun to write in America during the years when Hulme was developing his aesthetic in England. He arrived in London after the Imagist movement was under way, became associated with its members temporarily, and learned of their doctrine chiefly through their discarded leader, Ezra Pound. Eliot never met Hulme, and although through Pound, through study of the appendix to *Ripostes,* and perhaps through Hulme's articles in *The New Age,* he could have known something of Hulme's poetic theory, it is not likely that he was closely acquainted with it until the publication of *Speculations* in 1924.

Nevertheless, his early poems, including "The Love Song of J. Alfred Prufrock," written before he could have known anything of Hulme, best accomplish the task Hulme outlined as the responsibility of the modern poet. It would seem reasonable to suggest that Eliot's verse approximated Hulme's because his aesthetic was based upon the same fundamental philosophical assumptions, but such a theory cannot here be more than tentative. The poetry and prose that Eliot published before 1918 reveal only the most unsubstantial clues to his philosophy; this work does include the essay, "Tradition and the Individual Talent," but the emphasis here is primarily literary, and, as Mr. Matthiessen has pointed out, the first indication of the constructive thought that was developing from the despair of the earlier poems was given in 1926. In this year, he defined a "modern tendency . . . toward something which, for want of a better name, we may call classicism."[4] He included Hulme's *Speculations*, with five other books, as clearly illustrating the tendency toward a classical attitude, which had enlisted his sympathies. Since Eliot ultimately reached a philosophical position similar to the one expressed in *Speculations*, the attitude of the early poems may well share the same irony and disillusion over human limitations which led Hulme to formulate his theory of the religious attitude and a classical aesthetic consistent with it.

Eliot, however, took poetry's mission much more seriously than did Hulme, and even this verse cannot be too closely associated with Imagism or an Imagist aesthetic. His use of image and metaphor looked toward his later definition of the objective correlative, which aims at fullness of expression and communication rather than merely virtuosity and owes more to Pound's "equations" for the emotions than to Hulme's image. Yet *Prufrock and Other Observa-*

4 "The Idea of a Literary Review," *The New Criterion*, Vol. IV, No. 1 (January, 1926), 5.

tions achieves a greater significance than any verse published under the Imagist label, which cannot be explained by saying that he took poetry more seriously than they did, nor by arguing that the Imagists were hampered by a set of rules to which they had to write, for Eliot's early poems satisfy all of the demands of the manifestoes. It is only in actual practice that a possible explanation appears. "Oread" and "In a Station of the Metro" employ the single image and assume that, once established effectively, it can stand upon its beauty, or its specially perceived characteristics, upon its intrinsic interest; Eliot employed a series of images, each interesting but finding its full meaning only as a part of the effect of the poem as a whole—and the poem is not just delicately colored pictures or a series of sensations, but pictures and sensations which become a commentary on the society and experience which produced it. This is not to say that faces in a Metro station should have inspired Pound or any other Imagist to comment upon the social scene; it is only to say that their likeness to "petals on a wet, black bough" elicits from the reader merely an admiration for the poet's visualizing and linguistic power, and to suggest that the experience and sensibility communicated by his poem are not of enough complexity and importance to give it major stature.

Yet Imagism has served poets less closely associated with it, offering them what it offered its own—a discipline in conciseness of expression. Poets like William Carlos Williams, Marianne Moore, Wallace Stevens, and Hart Crane have also, in varying ways and degrees, found Imagism useful. Of these, Williams was closest to the school, through his early friendship with Pound and H. D. and his contribution to *Des Imagistes*. And though he was largely ignored by Imagism thereafter, his poetry is often closer to what seemed to be the Imagist ideal than any in the three later anthologies. One quality that has always dominated his work is its objectivity: he has tried to bring the word as close as possible to the object, cutting away any conventional, sentimental, too human associations it might have. He is interested in objects, using language to reproduce their appearance as concisely, exactly, scientifically, as possible. He *presents* his material in a way that Pound approved:

BETWEEN WALLS

the back wings
of the

hospital where
nothing

will grow lie
cinders

in which shine
the broken

pieces of a green
bottle

Yet there is often in his choice of objects a comment which is stronger for its being unstated; for all their detachment "The Young Housewife" and "The Poor" go far beyond Imagism in their implications, and "The Yachts" may be read as an expression of the fully developed, humanitarian sympathy which underlies Williams' poetry.

Richard Aldington claimed discovery of Marianne Moore, though she never approached the Imagist circle any more closely than this. Yet there is much in her poetry also that could be called Imagism: its obsession with exactness of detail, with clarity of impression, with making the object real, even though it appear in a context created by the poetic imagination. She chooses to write about an object, however, because she finds in it certain characteristics whose significance extends beyond the object. In the snail, for example, she finds that *"Contractility is a virtue/ as modesty is a virtue"* and the snail is held up as example to writers, illustrating qualities stylistically desirable. Thus, while she perhaps offers greater objectivity than Williams, she paradoxically achieves it without the complete exclusion of the poet that one associates with Imagism.

Wallace Stevens, with Williams and Marianne Moore, was a principal contributor to *Others*, a magazine criticized by Amy Lowell as too radical in its tastes. Certain of his poems may be called Imagistic; "Study of Two Pears," for example, is a still life which expresses shape, color, the reality of things that is so important a part of his aesthetic. His attention to metaphor, his use of color, his fastidiousness in selecting the materials of poetry also recall the Imagist; but Stevens' poetry is perhaps less Imagistic than that of any of these three writers who began their careers in an aesthetic climate conditioned by Imagist manifestoes and poetry. His interest is in the world of actuality, and in the extent to which the imagination can transform this world; but this interest has led him to poetic speculation on broad questions of religion and aesthetics.

For these writers Imagism offered instructive examples of one way in which modern poetry, through objectivity, exactness, natural diction and rhythms might regain strength and freshness of expression; it was a means to their own ends, sometimes carrying a poem by itself, though such poems seem only exercises, preparing for more ambitious work where Imagism disappears in a wholly original style. For a poet like Hart Crane, further removed from the immediate sphere of Imagism, its principles served a similar but more limited function. Two or three early poems clearly follow Imagist models, and after these there are only isolated examples like "March" which concentrate upon the narrow Imagist ideal: *The Bridge* has its own style through which it would be pointless to try to trace Imagist technique. One could continue with other more or less conscious echoes of Imagism in the writing of major contemporary poets, but these should indicate its importance and the necessary limitations of its influence: modern poetry is better off for this early effort to redefine and reinvigorate the word, to teach the poet to write a good line.

In the early thirties, of course, there was a momentary revival of interest. René Taupin's study appeared in 1929; Glenn Hughes brought out an Imagist anthology in 1930 and his book on the movement the next year. It was during 1931 also that the Objectivists attracted some notice, in which Imagism shared, for the Objectivists proposed not only to correct certain weaknesses of the earlier doctrine but to reassert what in it had proved most useful. As Objectivists, William Carlos Williams and others criticized Imagism's formal, structural weaknesses, and while praising again accuracy of detail, insisted that this mark of artistic integrity was not enough, that the detail must contribute to an over-all pattern which would give the poem an existence of its own. Their criticism was thus only another indication that as anything more than a healthy example for the writer Imagism had little to offer.

The publication of the manifestoes was a signal that marked the setting in motion of a new period in poetry, and, whether one agreed with the Imagists or attacked them, he was, if at all concerned with poetry, almost inevitably forced to a new awareness of its problems and resources. Imagism showed that a few poets at least were attempting to redefine it in such a way that it could continue to exist as a difficult and exacting medium worth serious study. In defining certain fundamentals of poetic expression and drawing attention to them, Imagism rendered a general service in breaking up old forms and momentarily reducing poetry to essentials. The *vers libre* controversy which redirected attention to the unit of measure certainly owed much of its vigor to the part played by the Imagists, though it would be too much to say that they introduced free verse to modern poets: Sandburg and Lindsay, for example, developed their own rhythms, as did Eliot.

Much more significant was their focus upon the directness and originality to be achieved by selection of the apt image or metaphor, an accomplishment that can be attributed to their own example and to the examples provided by the French poets they did so much to publicize. Perhaps most significant of all was the stimulus that they gave to the experimental attitude toward art, a stimulus which has had its result in the remarkable achievements of modern American poetry. In a period that seemed to have lost sympathy for verse, their work was valuable, and, though succeeding poets have found the implied limitations of Imagist technique too confining (as did the Imagists themselves), the Imagist attitude toward the materials of poetry and the function of the poet provided one basis for the more complex theories that were to take its place.

Index

Le Problème du style: 82, 83, 183

Les Illuminations: 177

Lewis, Wyndham: 14, 18, 19, 20, 45, 48, 160, 187, 190, 198, 199, 201, 202, 203, 212

Lindsay, Vachel: 44, 225

L'Influence du symbolisme français: 76, 95 n.

Little Review, The: 33, 42, 44, 45, 75, 85, 175

Lowell, Amy: 11, 16, 17, 18, 21–24, 44, 45, 47, 89, 91, 96, 97, 98, 101, 102, 111, 120, 121, 143, 144, 146, 147, 157, 163, 178, 180, 181, 183, 185, 188, 216, 217, 223; as leader of Imagism, 26–38; and *vers libre,* 99–100; and Imagist theory, 170–75

Lowes, J. L.: 36

Loy, Mina: 216

Mallarmé, Stéphane: 8, 76, 78, 79, 80, 81, 102, 112, 132

Marinetti, F. T.: 44, 190, 197, 198, 199, 212; and Futurist theory, 191–95

Marsden, Dora: 12, 44

Marsh, Edward: 17

Martial: 161

Masters, Edgar Lee: 36, 41, 43, 44

Mathews, Elkin: 15

Matthiessen, F. O.: 220

Mirrors of Illusion: 105

Monro, Harold: 11, 15, 18, 26, 32, 34, 35

Monroe, Harriet: 4, 7–11, 12, 15, 16, 26, 32, 35, 36 n., 39, 42, 44, 74, 85, 114, 136, 145, 161, 176, 187

Moore, Marianne: 29, 34, 221, 222–23

Moréas, Jean: 76

Nevinson, C. R. W.: 6 n., 50, 197

Date Due

DEC 1 1982			
FEB 2 2 1988			
DEC 20			
NOV 2 0 1995			